GOD A

together with
'Sinners in the hands of an angry God'

SIGNS OF TRUE REVIVAL

GOD AT WORK?

SIGNS OF TRUE REVIVAL

An easier to read and abridged version of
'The Distinguishing Marks of a Work of the Spirit of God'
by Jonathan Edwards

The full version is available from
The Banner of Truth Trust
Edinburgh EH12 6EL

Prepared by Gary Benfold
Pastor of Limes Avenue Baptist Church,
AYLESBURY

Joint Managing Editors
J.P. Arthur M.A.
H.J. Appleby

©GRACE PUBLICATIONS TRUST
139 Grosvenor Avenue
London, N5 2NH,
England

First published 1995

ISBN 0 946462 38 0

Distributed by: EVANGELICAL PRESS
12 Wooler Street
Darlington
Co. Durham DL1 1RQ
England

Printed in Great Britain by
Cox & Wyman Ltd, Reading.

Cover design: L.L. Evans

Contents

Section 3: some practical inferences

*****

Bible references are taken from
the New International Version

Foreword

It is now more than two hundred years since Jonathan Edwards preached the sermon which forms the bulk of this book. The circumstances under which he preached are interesting enough to make the continued republication more than worthwhile; yet that is not the reason why this book is produced. Edwards preached this sermon and then went on to publish it because he was concerned that his fellow Christians did not seem to know how they were to recognise God's work. If that was true in his day, it is even more true now.

From time to time we hear of strange things happening in God's church. Some people immediately welcome these things, and go searching for them themselves; others immediately condemn them. Both groups may well be guilty of the same lack of discernment. Let me explain.

The Situation in Edwards' Day.
Jonathan Edwards was Pastor of the Congregational Church in Northampton, New England. Although his ministry, and that of his predecessor (and grandfather) Solomon Stoddard, had been greatly blessed, by the year 1740 it was the general opinion that the state of true Christianity in the area was very low. Yet in 1740 the situation began to change, and it soon became obvious to many that God was doing a great work in the area. By the end of May that year it was already being spoken of as the greatest revival yet experienced in America. A visit of the great evangelist George Whitefield, in October of the same year, was a considerable help. But Whitefield only stayed ten days, and even after he left religious concern continued to grow. Large numbers of people came under great conviction of sin, and many of them then moved on to rejoice in God's salvation. Then, in 1742, the revival gradually began

to spread to surrounding areas, and 'As Spring passed into Summer in 1741, no one could well keep track of the number of places which were witnessing the revival. Churches which in some cases had been cold and dry at the beginning of the year were transformed before the end.' [1]

On the 8th of July that year (1741) Jonathan Edwards preached at nearby Enfield. So far, Enfield had not been touched by the revival, and the people seemed very happy about that. Edwards preached his now-famous sermon 'Sinners in the hands of an angry God' which is also included in this volume. The effect was terrific. By the end of the sermon many people - if not all - were 'bowed down with an awful conviction of their sin and danger.' Even before the sermon was over there was much moaning and crying from those in the congregation who felt their sin, and some were crying out 'What must I do to be saved?' Though it was a remarkable scene, Murray comments 'There were... many similar days in the year 1741.' [2]

This great revival was over by the end of 1743, but its effects were long lasting. Edwards and others were able to testify of considerable numbers -thousands - whose lives had been transformed and were (in the cautious language of the day) 'hopefully converted'. Surely, we would expect that all Christians would be rejoicing at what had happened.

But it was not so; in fact, there was considerable opposition. At first, the opposition had simply been silence; ministers had made no comment on the revival in such a pointed way that their opposition to it was becoming obvious to all. By 1742, the opposition was more open, and there was strong debate. A letter of 89 pages, with a lengthy introduction, was published anonymously. In it the revival was seen as mere fanaticism, and in particular the writer of the introduction took strong opposition to the remarkable bodily effects that the revival was producing. To his mind, there could be no possible connection between such things and the work of the Holy Spirit. Those 'bodily effects' had begun to show themselves in 1741. Jonathan

Edwards preached at a private house in May of that year, and one or two of the congregation 'were so greatly affected with a sense of the greatness and glory of divine things' that it overcame their strength 'having a very visible effect upon their bodies.' Later, such scenes were to become common, and became the basis - or perhaps the excuse - for a great deal of criticism. Some were critical of the revival because it made Christianity the subject of common conversation. Others tried to explain it away; the emotion, they said, was caused by the vivid preaching about hell; people were simply terrified. Then, they argued, some people were merely copying what they had seen others do, and a kind of mass hysteria was spreading. Such things were regarded as proof that the Holy Spirit was not at work. It is to these people that Edwards replied in 'The Distinguishing Marks', and he deals with their objections. First, he lists nine things which, he argues, do not prove anything. Then he lists five things which, he says, the Scriptures say are sure and certain marks that the Holy Spirit is at work. Finally, he makes a thorough application - all (apparently) in the course of one sermon! We may well be surprised by the idea of a sermon like this (or, indeed, of sermons like these; 'Sinners in the Hands of an Angry God' has a similar structure.) It is true that Edwards' day was very different from ours, and his people much more used to closely-reasoned sermons. We must not forget this; at the same time, preachers need to be careful not to use it too readily as an excuse! More thought, more logic, more structure, more imagery, more application would do a lot to improve our pulpits - and, perhaps, be used by God in bringing about another Great Awakening.

The situation today.

We too live in days when true Christianity is in a poor state. For the most part, there are few real conversions in our churches; even worse, nobody seems to mind very much. Then, from time to time, we hear remarkable reports of strange things happening.

Just as in Edwards' day, those strange things have their critics; often, the arguments they use are exactly the same as those used by Edwards' opponents. 'It is just mass hysteria; it has nothing to do with the Holy Spirit.'

There are, however, other voices being heard, voices which are prepared to accept anything new and apparently powerful as obviously from God; no tests are applied, no discernment is used. Even to question what is happening is regarded as (very nearly) blasphemy against the Holy Spirit.

Edwards' work answers both viewpoints better than anything else. We desperately need to learn the lessons he can teach us. If God really is at work in new and powerful ways, we need to know it. We need to sweep aside prejudice and rejoice at God's mercy among us. But if he is not at work - if there is some other (perhaps sinister) explanation of what is happening, we need to know that too. We cannot afford to be gullible. How can we know? Edwards will tell us; he will warn us what not to base our judgement on; he will show us how to make a proper judgement. For that reason, this book has been produced. Edwards' words have been updated as gently as possible; but his arguments have been left intact.

While this book was in production, Edwards' name has surfaced again in the churches; his contribution has been recognised and admired, and statements have been produced which point us to these tests once more. Yet, probably because Edwards himself is difficult for the modern reader, it seems to me that he has been misunderstood. Conclusions have been drawn as if they have his support which are actually contrary to his views. In particular, he is quoted as if he regards these tests as authenticating strange phenomena. But he never draws that conclusion; his work needs to be read again and I hope that this book will make that possible for many people who would never otherwise read Edwards at all.

Can we trust Edwards? Yes, we can. Not because he was one of the greatest minds America has ever produced, but because he turns us to the Scriptures. They alone are able to shine light in our darkness; they will tell us how we are to judge. These criteria will be valid in each and every situation; whether now (two hundred years after Edwards' death) or two hundred years from now, when we too are dead and long forgotten.

It is my conviction that one of the greatest needs in the Christian church today is discernment; and that that need will only grow as the years progress. May God bless to us again the words of his servant Edwards as we are led into the Scriptures; and to God alone be glory now and evermore.

G. B.

[1] Iain H. Murray, 'Jonathan Edwards, A New Biography' (Banner of Truth, 1987) p. 166
[2] ibid, p.169

Introduction

In our day everyone seems to be talking about the Holy Spirit, and arguing over his work. Yet few people seem to know how to recognise when the Spirit is at work at all, how to tell the true from the false. This book is written to help.

No age has ever seen more of the power of the Holy Spirit than the days of the Apostles. His miraculous gifts were seen in great abundance; he was also at work convincing large numbers of men and women of sin and making them holy disciples of Christ.

At the same time, the devil was equally active producing false miracles and false gospels. The New Testament makes it clear again and again that there were imitators of God's work all around. For this reason it was absolutely necessary that Christ's church should be given rules and clear marks of God's work, so that Christians would be able to tell the true from the false and not be led astray. One chapter of the New Testament is particularly devoted to this issue, and that is 1 John chapter 4. More fully than any other chapter in the Bible this one tells us how to recognise when God really is at work. The apostle John gives us several ways of recognising the true work of the Spirit to make absolutely sure that no-one misunderstands him. He does so clearly enough to enable us to use his rules safely in our own churches. It is surprising therefore that people do not pay more attention to this chapter today; so many mistakes could have been avoided.

John begins by mentioning that we know we are Christ's when his Spirit dwells in us. 'Those who obey his commands live in him and he in them. And this is how we know that he lives in us: We know it by the Spirit he gave us.' (3:23) From this we understand that the apostle does not just want us to know how to tell a true prophecy from a false prophecy, or a

God-given miracle from a false one. He also wants us to recognise when the Spirit is at work in his people saving them and giving them greater maturity in Christ. This will be even more obvious to us when we look at the things he says.

First though, before John tells us how we may recognise the true from the false, he warns us about two things.

The first warning is this; we must not be too ready to believe anything that claims to be a true work of the Spirit. 'Dear friends, do not believe every spirit, but test the spirits to see whether they are from God.' (4:1) Not everything that *claims* to be God at work really *is* God at work; and it is important to understand this.

The second warning is that there are many false powers: 'because many false prophets have gone out into the world.' (4:1) These people not only pretend to have great revelations from God but also to be among heaven's favourite people, more holy than others! This verse commands us to examine both claims. Sadly, we cannot just believe what people say; nor can we assume that every power at work is God's power.

So, using this chapter, I want to show you what are reliable proofs that God is at work, so that we may correctly judge anything that happens to us or to others. We must realise that God has given the Bible to guide us in spiritual things; it infallibly tells us all we need to know. We need not be afraid to trust the rules God has given; the Holy Spirit inspired the Bible, and knows enough to recognise his own work! He has also given us enough guidance to help us recognise his work too.

As I said earlier, the Spirit sets out to give us these rules in this chapter more completely than anywhere else. In this present book therefore I will not examine other Scriptures to see what rules they give us; I shall limit myself to this chapter. It is sufficient, and I think we will find it a great help.

But because this current revival has attracted much criticism, I cannot start with things that prove that God *is* at work. People point at some of the things that are happening and say

'That proves that God is not at work; the revival is therefore false.' That is a serious charge to make, and I must answer it. So first of all I will look at some of the things that have been quoted as proof that this revival is false, and show that they prove no such thing! In fact I will show that they prove nothing at all, good or bad. They do not prove that God *is* at work (though some are ready to claim that they do) and they do not prove that a work is false (though some claim that they do).

What are these things that prove nothing?

Section 1:

Things that prove nothing one way or the other

1. When unusual things are happening

It does not prove that an experience or a revival is false just because unusual things are happening, provided that the rules of Scripture are not broken. We cannot just say "The church is not used to this" because God may work in new and extraordinary ways. He has done so before (to the surprise of men and angels) - and we have no reason to assume that he has stopped doing so now. Scripture says that God will, in the future, do things that have never been seen before. The Holy Spirit is sovereign: he uses a great variety of means to accomplish his work. Although he will not break the rules he has given, he may work in a greater variety of ways than we realise. We must not limit God where he does not limit himself.

So it does not prove that an experience is false if people's minds are influenced in an unusual manner. They may have a very strong conviction of how awful sin is or a great sense of how miserable it is to be without Christ. They may have a great realisation of the certainty and glory of divine things and so be emotionally moved in remarkable ways - to fear or sorrow, desire, love or joy. Many people may be affected like this at the same time - even very young ones. Yet these things do not contradict the Scriptures and so are not proof that what is happening is false. In fact, quite the reverse - an unusual amount of power is an argument that God is at work, provided the Scriptures are not broken.

Many people - especially the elderly - tend to be prejudiced against anything new. If it did not happen in their fathers' days, they think, it must be wrong! But if this argument were true it would apply in the days of the apostles. In their days, God's work was carried on in completely new ways and with greater power than ever. Never before had so many people been transformed suddenly by the Holy Spirit. Never before had so many people shown such great zeal, or whole towns, cities and countries known such changes. The work was so unusual that the Jews were amazed, and could hardly believe that God was at work. Sometimes, they thought the persons involved had gone mad - Acts 2:13, 26:24 and 1 Cor 4:10.

Furthermore, we have reason to believe from Scripture that the last ever revival before the end of the world will be even greater. In those days people will cry out with amazement 'Who has ever heard of such a thing? Who has ever seen such things? Can a country be born in a day or a nation be brought forth in a moment? Yet no sooner is Zion in labour than she gives birth to her children.' (Is. 66:8) If God is going to do such extraordinary things, we may assume that he will do them in extraordinary ways.

2. There are unusual effects on people's bodies

We cannot tell whether God is at work by the effects on a person's body. Suppose people weep or tremble, groan or cry out; or they experience bodily pains or lack of strength. We cannot conclude from these things that God is at work, nor can we conclude that he is not. Why not? Because Scripture nowhere tells us to pass judgement on this basis. The Bible does not teach that such bodily effects are a mark of the Spirit's work and the Bible does not tell us that these things mean he is not at work. It is vitally important that we learn to make judgements on the right basis - that is, Scripture not prejudice. Scripture does not exclude such bodily effects when God's Spirit is at work.

18

When these things do occur, three things will help us to understand what is happening. These three things are *first,* the nature of divine things; *second* the nature of man and *third* the laws of the union between soul and body.

Let us imagine a man who has begun to understand how real God and eternity are. Should we be surprised if he cries out, or feels weak and faint, or even experiences bodily pains? Not unless we are very ignorant! For example, we all realise that the misery of hell is so awful that any one who saw that reality clearly would find it more than he could bear. If at the same time that man saw *himself* in danger of that hell; if he did not know whether he could escape it and even felt that he might go there at any moment - then this would be even more true. Human nature is such that whenever a man sees himself in danger of great calamity, he expects it to happen straight away. We see this in times of war for example, when even a shaking leaf can make men tremble. At such times men's hearts are full of fear; they expect the enemy to arrive at any moment. The time of their own death seems to have come. In the same way if a man begins to see the reality of hell he expects to go there straight away! He sees that he is hanging by a slender thread over a fiery pit with the thread ready to snap. He knows that many people have been in the same position earlier, and most of them have fallen and perished. He can see nothing within reach to take hold of and save himself. He knows that he is in the hands of God - and God is angry with him because of his sin. Are we surprised that he is terrified? Of course he will cry out in those circumstances!

We should not be surprised if this glimpse of God's anger takes away his strength so that he becomes weak or faints. In the same way a man's strength may be taken away when he catches a glimpse of the glory of the Lord Jesus Christ and the greatness of his dying love. We all admit that no man can see God and live, and that our mortal bodies could stand no more than the smallest taste of the glory and love of Christ. (The saints in heaven, of course, know much more.) God sometimes

19

gives his saints real foretastes of heaven; it is not surprising therefore if they are made to feel faint. The queen of Sheba fainted when she saw the glory of Solomon. Why should we be surprised if the church faints at the glory of Christ? We must expect to see more of this in that prosperous, peaceful and glorious kingdom which Christ will set up in the world in its last age.

Some people object to such things though because we have no examples of them in the New Testament. This is not true; but even if it were, it would not prove anything. Scripture does not *exclude* such things; neither does reason. The New Testament does not speak of any one weeping, groaning or sighing through fear of hell or a sense of God's anger. Yet we know that, when we see people in such a state, it is the work of the Spirit of God. Why? Because these things fit in well with what we know of human nature and what the Scripture does say about the convicting work of the Spirit. There is no need for anything to be said about these external effects.

Anyway, as I have said, it is not true that we have no examples of such things in the New Testament. The Philippian jailer is one example. In distress and amazement he came trembling and fell down before Paul and Silas. He did not do this deliberately, as if to beg something from Paul and Silas. The first thing he says to them is 'Sirs, what must I do to be saved?' (Acts 16:29,30.) His falling down and his trembling seem to have been caused by his deep sense of need. The Psalmist tells us how he suffered bodily weakness and cried out when his conscience convinced him of sin: 'When I kept silence my bones wasted away through my groaning all day long. For day and night your hand was heavy upon me; my strength was sapped as in the heat of summer.' (Psalm 32:3, 4) We may at least deduce from this that such things may happen. Even if we think the psalmist is using a figure of speech, a hyperbole, yet that figure of speech must mean something! The disciples saw Christ coming to them through the storm, and cried out for fear. (Mt. 14:26) Why then should we think it strange if a man cries out in fear when he has begun to understand that he is God's enemy and is in great danger of eternal misery? The bride speaks of herself as overpowered with the love of Christ, making her faint. 'Strengthen me with raisins, refresh me with apples, for I am faint with love.' (Song 2:5) 'O daughters of Jerusalem, I charge you - if you find my lover, what will you tell him? Tell him I am faint with love.' (5:8) We may at least argue from these Scriptures that such things can happen in the church of Christ.

Some argue against these things because, they say, the same things happen to all sorts of heretical fanatics. What a ridiculous argument! To prove that heretics in the past have trembled hardly proves that Paul and the jailer were not trembling from real conviction. In fact all such arguments seem to be exceedingly silly; people who argue like this are walking in the dark. They do not know where they stand or how they are supposed to make judgements. The important thing is to get at the root cause of such effects, to understand human nature and then examine the effects by the rule of Scripture.

3. There is much talk about religion.

It is no proof that a work is false if it causes a great deal of debate about religion. Some people are suspicious of this revival because everyone is talking about it! Those who object say true religion is quiet and secret. It cannot be seen. Now of course it is true that true religion is not like the Pharisees (boastful and showy), but true religion may cause a lot of excitement and interest. In fact, human nature being what it is, it is impossible that there should be a powerful work of God without this happening. When people are very anxious about their souls; when their hearts are moved and their minds are powerfully affected, people are bound to talk - and change! Obviously to say that people's minds are not being affected by God's Spirit just because they are greatly moved would be silly. Spiritual and eternal issues are so great and of such infinite importance that it is absurd for men to be 'moderately moved' by them. Whenever people are greatly affected by anything, there will be noise and even commotion. Human nature demands it.

Yes, Christ does say 'The kingdom of God does not come with your careful observation.' (Lk. 17:20) He means that his kingdom is not outward and visible. It is not like earthly kingdoms, set up with great pomp and in particular places. As Christ explains in his next words, you cannot travel somewhere to see it. 'Nor will people say 'Here it is' or 'There it is' because the kingdom of God is within you.' But this does not mean that Satan's kingdom will be overthrown and Christ's kingdom set up without any observable effect! There will be a mighty change in things, to astonish the whole world. This is prophesied in Scripture - even by Christ himself in this very place. He explains his earlier words 'For the Son of Man in his day will be like lightning, which flashes and lights up the sky from one end to the other.' (vs. 24) False Christs will come privately and secretly; but when the true Christ returns, the Kingdom of God will be set up publicly. The whole world will see it; like lightning that cannot be hid it glares in everyone's eyes and shines from one side of heaven to the other. When Christ's kingdom came with the great gift of the Spirit at Pentecost, it caused a great deal of excitement and interest everywhere. When the Spirit came there was even great opposition in Jerusalem, Samaria, Antioch, Ephesus, Corinth and other places. True religion filled the world with commotion, so that some said the apostles had turned the world upside down. (Acts 17:6)

4. There are unusual effects on peoples' imaginations.

It does not prove that a work is false if many people have great impressions made on their imaginations. This does not prove that these people have nothing else.

When many people of different types have their minds and hearts strongly occupied with invisible things, strong impressions on the imagination are inevitable. Again, it is human nature: we cannot think of invisible things without a degree of imagination. Try it! Even if you are a person of great intellectual ability, you will not be able to concentrate on God, or Christ, or the eternal world, without imaginary ideas intruding. The harder you concentrate, the more your mind and heart is occupied and moved, then the stronger those imaginary ideas will be. The tendency is even more marked when people are surprised by their thoughts. When fear or joy takes strong hold of a person; when they have changed suddenly from an opposite extreme (for example, from a dread terror to a ravished delight) then the imagination may be particularly strong. So it is no wonder that people are not able to distinguish very well between what is imaginary and what is intellectual and spiritual. Such people may give too much weight to their imaginations and we should not be surprised at that. Nor must we be surprised if they speak too much of these things when giving their testimonies. If they have little spiritual understanding or discernment this is quite likely to happen.

God has given us imaginations. He also made our nature such that we cannot think of spiritual and invisible things without using our imaginations. If used properly and kept under control our imaginations can be very helpful. It is also true that, if the imagination is too strong, it can be a great hindrance rather than a help, but I know of many people where it is plain that God has really made use of the imagination for his own purposes. This is especially the case with the poorly educated. God seems to come down to their level and deal with them as with very young children. (Just as in the Old Testament, when the church was very young, he instructed it by types and outward representations.) I can see nothing unreasonable in this. Let others with much experience of dealing with enquiring and concerned souls judge for themselves.

In some cases people have experienced great spiritual ecstasy. This does not prove that God is not at work! Some people do seem to be very strongly moved by visions of heaven and sights of glory. I have known some such instances, and can see no need to assume that they are of the devil. But we do not have to assume either that they are the same kind of thing as the prophets' visions, or St. Paul's rapture into Paradise. All we need to account for these things is to understand what happens when human nature is greatly moved. I have already shown that people with a proper understanding of the greatness of spiritual matters and the beauty and love of Christ may well be overpowered by it. So when great numbers are given such understanding, it is not surprising that some amongst them have their imaginations stimulated! It is no surprise when thoughts are so intense and full of Christ - when the whole soul is so ravished - that other parts of the body are affected as well, even as far as being deprived of strength and ready to faint. Should we be surprised that, in these cases, the brains of some people (those who are most easily affected by such things) should be so moved that all strength should be diverted to the mind, and the imaginations?

Some attach too much importance to these things, regarding them as prophetic visions or divine revelations, or sometimes hints from heaven of what will soon happen. When this is the case, in some instances I have known, they have proved to be wrong. But still I think that these things are sometimes from the Holy Spirit, though indirectly. What I mean is that their extraordinary frame of mind, their strong sense of God (which produces such imaginations) is from the Spirit. If the mind continues to think holy thoughts, and continues to have a high value of spiritual things even to rapture - these things are from the Spirit of God. But the imaginations which accompany it are accidental and so will contain things that are confused, improper, and false.

5. Many people are influenced by the examples of others.

It does not prove that a work is false if people are greatly influenced by the examples of others. We know that God uses means to carry on his work in the world, and I can show that this means may be from God as much as others. There are two ways of proving this:

First, it is Scriptural. The Bible tells us that people are influenced by the good example of others, and we are actually commanded to set good examples because of this. (Mt. 5:16, 1 Pet. 3:1, 1 Tim 4:12, Titus 2:7) It also commands us to be influenced by others, and to follow them. (2 Cor 8:1-7, Heb. 6:12, Phil. 3:17, 1 Cor 4:16, 11:1, 2 Thess 3:9, 1 Thess. 1:7) So the use of example is one way God uses to accomplish his purposes. How can it prove that God is not at work that one of his own ways of working is used!

Second, it is reasonable. Just as our minds may receive truth from the words of another person, so also we may be influenced - and even more strongly - by their example. Words are used to convey our own ideas to others; but actions sometimes do that much more fully. It is wrong therefore to argue that an effect is not good because the people have been affected by what they see happening to others.

Even if no words are spoken a person may be influenced solely by seeing others affected if it is obvious what they are affected by. When a person sees another suffering great bodily pain he may have a much clearer idea of what is being suffered than words could ever produce. In the same way, he might receive a greater idea of excellent and delightful things from the behaviour of one that is enjoying them, than any words could produce. Think about it: is this not true? Nor is it only weak and ignorant people who are influenced by example. Many who have very strong reasoning powers are also influenced. Not only that: they will be more easily influenced by reasoned argument backed up by examples, than by reasoned argument on its own. Surely this is obvious. Some say that

25

when the religious affections are raised by this means, the effect proves flashy and soon vanishes. That may be so, and Christ speaks of stony-ground hearers. But it is also true that the affections of some raised by this means do last and produce the salvation of the person concerned.

There has never been a great revival yet where the example of others was not a great influence on people. It was true at the Reformation, and anyone who reads the Acts of the Apostles will know it was true there. Not only were individuals influenced by other individuals, but one city or town was influenced by another. 'And so you became a model to all the believers in Macedonia and Achaia.' (1Thess 1:7,8)

Some people object that the Scriptures speak of *the word* being the main way God's work is done, not example. But this is not a valid argument. The word of God is the main way by which other methods operate and are made effective. Even the sacraments have no effect except by the word. Example is only effective when the word of God instructs and guides the mind. Without that, everything that the eye sees means nothing. It is the word of God that is held out and applied by example, just as the word of the Lord sounded to other towns in Macedonia and Achaia by the example of those in Thessalonica who believed.

Scripture does teach in many places that example is a major means of extending the church of God. One example is Ruth. Ruth followed Naomi out of the land of Moab into the land of Israel, having made up her mind that she would not leave her. Instead, Ruth decided to go where Naomi went, and to stay where Naomi stayed. (Ruth 1:16) Naomi's people would be Ruth's people, and Naomi's God would be Ruth's God. Ruth was ancestor to both David and Christ, and her story is included in the Bible because she is a type or picture of the church. When she leaves the land of Moab and its gods, and comes to the land and trusts the God of Israel, we have a type or picture of the conversion of the Gentile church. In fact, it is a picture of the conversion of every sinner, for we are all naturally aliens and strangers to God and his people. When we are converted we leave our own people and our father's house, and become fellow-citizens with the saints and true Israelites. The same power of example is taught by the effect of the bride on the daughters of Jerusalem. First, they are awakened by seeing her in such extraordinary circumstances; then they are converted. (Song 5:8,9 and 6:1) This is undoubtedly one way that 'the Spirit and the Bride say, come.' (Rev. 22:17) John means the Spirit in the bride, the church. The Bible prophecies that God's work will be carried on in this way in the last outpouring of the Spirit that will introduce the glorious day of the church. Scripture often speaks of this: for example, Zech. 8:21-23.

6. There is some unwise and irregular conduct

The Spirit may be at work even though some people who are affected are guilty of unwise and irregular conduct. Let us remember that God pours out his Spirit to make men holy, not to make them diplomats! In any mixed crowd, where there are some who are wise and some who are not, some who are young and some who are old, some who are less able and others that are more able, some will behave unwisely. This is especially true when they are under strong impressions of mind. Very few people know how to behave properly when affected by any strong emotion, whether spiritual or natural. To do so requires a great deal of discretion, strength and steadiness of mind. But a thousand unwise acts does not prove that a work is false. In fact, even the presence of things directly contrary to the Scriptures, God's Word, does not prove the case. Human nature is weak, and we all have a great deal of darkness and sin still within us, even when God has saved us. That is all the explanation we need.

In the New Testament we have at least one very clear example of such things, and that is the church at Corinth. The Spirit of God was powerfully present in those days of the apostles, and that is particularly so at Corinth. There is hardly a church in the New Testament more famous for the powerful work of the Spirit; sinners were saved and miraculous gifts abounded. Yet they could not be called a wise church! We know that they were unwise, sinful and confused, even in such things as the Lord's Supper and church discipline! In addition, they lacked proper respect in worship, they disagreed strongly about their teachers and even managed to make God's miraculous gifts of tongues and prophecy an excuse for argument.

So if we see a lack of wisdom, and irregular behaviour, in those who are doing a work, it does not prove that the work itself is false. The apostle Peter himself was guilty of a sinful error in his behaviour. Though he was a great, holy and inspired apostle - one of the mightiest men God used to set up his church - yet he made a great mistake. Paul tells us about it: 'When Peter came to Antioch, I opposed him to his face, because he was clearly in the wrong. Before certain men came from James, he used to eat with the Gentiles. But when they arrived, he began to draw back and separate himself from the Gentiles because he was afraid of those who belonged to the circumcision group. The other Jews joined him in his hypocrisy, so that by their hypocrisy even Barnabas was led astray' (Gal. 2:11-13). If this man - such an important figure in the church, an apostle who is one of the foundations of the church - could make such a mistake, how can we be surprised if lesser men do?

In particular, we should not make too hasty a judgement on people just because they are too ready to assume other people to be unconverted. Again, this is easy to account for. They may be in error about how to recognise hypocrisy in others. They may not fully understand how varied the means are which the Spirit uses. They may fail to make proper allowance for weakness and sin left in the heart of every true saint. They may also fail to realise the extent of their own blindness and weakness and remaining sin, giving way (unknowingly) to the sin of spiritual pride. We all agree that truly converted and holy men do have a great degree of blindness and sin left - why then should we be surprised when it shows itself? It is sad but true that many holy men have made this mistake.

It is a horrible thing to be lukewarm in our faith; zeal is an excellent thing. Yet, more than all other Christian virtues, it is zeal that needs to be strictly watched and examined. Sin, and particularly the sin of pride, so easily become mixed with it. Every time of reformation and revival of zeal in God's church has had its instances of people becoming unnecessarily severe. In the days of the apostles, it was about unclean meats; Christians grew angry and condemned one another as not true Christians at all. But the apostle recognised that both were influenced by a true desire to be holy: 'He who eats meat, eats to the Lord, for he gives thanks to God; and he who abstains, does so to the Lord and gives thanks to God' (Rom 14:6). In Corinth, they had developed the habit of praising some ministers and condemning others, and their pride led to great arguments. Yet God was at work and his work was carried on in the most marvellous manner. Following this, while the early church was still growing and concerned for holiness, some Christians became far too zealous for church discipline towards those who strayed. However penitent and humble the offender became, some were not prepared to accept him back into the church! Then in the days of Constantine the Great, some Christians were so concerned about paganism that they began to persecute the pagans. The Reformation also saw too much severity and some persecution. Even the great Calvin was guilty here! In those days, when true religion was flourishing, there were many who were guilty of criticising and condemning others who disagreed on some points of theology. Let us not be too hasty to pass judgement when such things happen in our own day.

7. *There are some errors of judgement (or even Satanic delusions)*

The Spirit of God may be at work even if many mistakes are made. In fact there may even be some Satanic delusions present. However powerfully the Spirit is at work, he no longer guides us infallibly as he did the apostles. We cannot treat anyone, or anyone's doctrine, as an infallible guide for the church.

If at a time of great religious revival many delusions of Satan are present, it is not safe to conclude that God is absent! Jannes and Jambres worked false miracles in Egypt, yet God was there too, working miracles. In fact, the same persons may be influenced much by God's Spirit and still, in other things, be misled by the devil. If anyone thinks this cannot be true he needs to remember that there are many things in the life of every true believer that seem to contradict one another. Grace and sin dwell in the same heart; the old man and the new man live together in the same person; the Kingdom of God and the Kingdom of the devil exist together in the same heart for a while.

It is true that in this revival many godly people have been too ready to believe that every impulse and impression they get is a direct revelation from God. That has been true in past revivals as well. Sometimes they believe that God has revealed the future to them; sometimes they just believe that God has told them directly what to do. We may not conclude from these errors, though, that the revival is false.

8. *Some people fall into heresy or sin*

God may still be at work even if some who seemed most influenced fall away into great heresy or sin. There are always counterfeits; but some things are still true. We must always expect this at a time of reformation. This has been true throughout church history, in every great revival.

Even in the days of the apostles this was true; some fell into great heresy, others into great sin, even though it had seemed that the Spirit had been greatly at work in them. Their experience and their conduct were so convincing that they were accepted by everyone as true brothers and fellow workers. No-one suspected anything was wrong until they left the churches. Some of them were even teachers and officers in the church - yes, even blessed with miraculous gifts of the Spirit! (See Hebrews 6) One example of this was Judas, fully accepted among the other disciples. No-one suspected anything - until by betraying Jesus he betrayed himself. Jesus himself had treated him outwardly in every way as a true disciple; he called him an apostle, sent him out to preach the gospel and gave him miraculous gifts of the Spirit. Although Christ knew everything about Judas, he did not act as the all-knowing judge and searcher of hearts. Instead he set an example to ordinary ministers in the Christian church. By this example we learn that we must not pretend that we can see hearts, and not act as if we can. Instead, we must conduct our business by what is visible and open.

In the days following the apostolic age there were instances of great apostates, who had been highly regard as men full of God's grace. Nicholas, one of the seven deacons, may be an example. He was believed by the Christians in Jerusalem to be full of the Spirit. He was chosen out of the vast congregation to be a deacon for that reason (Acts 6:3,5). Afterwards, he fell away and became the leader of a sect of gross heretics guilty of vile practices; they are called Nicolaitans, after him. (Rev. 2:6, 15) At the time of the Reformation, great numbers joined the reformers for a while and yet later turned away to the greatest and silliest errors and vile practices.

One particular danger in times of great revival is that many who seem for a while to take part in it afterwards turn away into whimsical and extravagant errors. They boast of high degrees of spirituality and perfection and criticise everyone else as carnal. The Gnostics did that in the apostles' day, and several sects did that at the Reformation. So the reformers not only had to battle with the Roman Catholic church but also with those who claimed to have far more light. These groups criticised those who took their stand on Scripture, calling them 'literalist' and 'vowelist' - that is, implying that the Reformers only knew the word and letter of Scripture, but did not know the Spirit of God! Whenever the gospel light began to shine and overthrow Catholicism, such people always seemed to spring up, like weeds among wheat. As a result, many mocked and despised the Reformation, and criticised Luther for preaching a carnal gospel. Yet some of these wild men had at first been highly esteemed by the reformers.

The same happened in England, when true religion prospered between the days of Charles I and Oliver Cromwell. There were similar problems in New England, even in her purest days. The devil is always active, sowing tares; yet the work of the Holy Spirit may be gloriously carried on.

9. There is much preaching about the horrors of hell

If ministers preach much about the terrors of God's holy law, with great earnestness and tenderness, God may still be at work.

Some people have objected that this is not a revival at all. They say that preachers are simply frightening people by preaching a lot about the terrors of God's holy law, and the fires of hell. But if there really is a hell of never-ending torments; and if many people are in great danger of going there, it is proper to warn them! If it is true that most people even in so-called 'Christian' countries go at last to hell because they had never given the matter any thought, it is proper to warn them! They must be told as much of the truth as possible. If I am in danger of going to hell, I want to know as much as I possibly can about how dreadful it is. If it seems that hell's reality does not matter to me, and so I am not trying to avoid it, the kindest man is the one who does most to warn me.

I ask you all - is not this the course you would take in a worldly calamity? Imagine your children in a house that is on fire. They are unaware of their danger, and even though you warn them, they pay no attention. Would you carry on warning them in a cold and heartless manner? Or would you cry aloud, in the most earnest terms you could, and warn them and plead with them? Of course you would! If you did otherwise, we would assume you were bereft of reason yourself. Men do not behave coldly and carelessly in important worldly matters which require great haste. They do not warn others of their danger in a cold and indifferent manner. We ministers claim to know what hell is; we say we have seen the condition of the damned and know how dreadful their case is. It is quite impossible therefore to avoid warning them and crying out to them.

If ministers preach of hell in a cold and unfeeling manner, their behaviour contradicts their words - even if those words are faithful to the facts. As I said before, actions have a language as well as words. We may *say* that men's danger is great, and their fate infinitely horrible. But if we are cold and unfeeling as we say it, we defeat our own purpose; the language of our actions is much louder than the language of our words.

Of course, I am not saying that we should only preach the law; it is quite possible not to give enough attention to other things. The gospel is to be preached as well as the law, and the law is to be preached only to make way for the gospel. The main work of ministers is to preach the gospel: 'Christ is the end of the law so that there may be righteousness for everyone who believes.' (Rom 10:4) A minister is very wrong if he preaches too much on the terrors of the law and so forgets his Lord and neglects to preach the gospel. Yet still, I say, the law must be insisted on, and the preaching of the gospel will be useless without it.

Let us not complain that the preachers in this revival are too fanatical! They are earnest, and a true earnestness is very beautiful. In fact, it is most appropriate to the nature of the subject. Yes, a preacher may be too boisterous. But some argue that it is wrong to frighten men into heaven; I would answer, that it is right to try and frighten people away from hell. Men do stand on the very edge of hell; they are about to fall in and are unaware of their danger. Is it not right to frighten a man out of a burning house? Some fears are quite reasonable!

Section 2:

Things that the Scriptures say prove that God is at work

Introduction

In the first section I have shown some negative signs - how we are not to judge a work. Now I intend to show how we may definitely conclude that God *is* at work. I want to show the signs which Scripture says are clear evidence that God is at work. We will then be able to use these signs to judge any work without fear of being misled.

As I said earlier, I propose to look only at those signs given in 1 John 4. That is because this chapter deals with this question plainly and more completely than any other part of the Bible. So let us look at the signs in the order they are given in the chapter.

1. When esteem for the true Jesus is raised

If a person's esteem of the true Jesus is raised it is a sure sign that the Spirit of God is at work. By 'the true Jesus' I mean this: that Jesus was born of a virgin and crucified outside the gates of Jerusalem; that he is the Son of God and the Saviour of men, as the gospel declares.

This sign is given by the apostle in the second and third verses. 'This is how you can recognise the Spirit of God: Every spirit that acknowledges that Jesus Christ has come in the flesh is from God, but every spirit that does not acknowledge Jesus is not from God.' This implies acknowledging more than that there was such a person as Jesus, who appeared in Palestine and did and suffered those things which the Bible says. It implies acknowledging that he was the Christ, that is, the Son of God, chosen to be Lord and Saviour. This is what the name Jesus Christ implies. We know that the apostle means this because of what he says in verse 15. He is still dealing with the same subject (the signs that the true Spirit is at work) and he says 'If anyone acknowledges that Jesus is the Son of God, God lives in him and he in God.'

This word 'acknowledge' is important. In the New Testament it means much more than merely 'admitting.' It implies knowing something and being willing to declare it in praise and love. For example, Mt. 10:32 says 'Whoever acknowledges me before men, I will also acknowledge him before my Father in heaven.' The same word is used in Rom 15:9, but translated 'praise': 'Therefore I will praise you among the Gentiles, I will sing hymns to your name.' Again, it is the same word in Phil 2:11, translated 'confess': 'every tongue (will) confess that Jesus Christ is Lord, to the glory of God the Father.' We can be sure that this is what John means here when we look at what he says in the next chapter, vs. 1: 'Everyone who believes that Jesus is the Christ is born of God.' The apostle Paul also confirms this when he gives the same rule to distinguish the true Spirit from all counterfeits in 1 Cor 12:3: 'Therefore I tell you that no-one who is speaking by the Spirit of God says "Jesus be cursed," and no-one can say "Jesus is Lord," except by the Holy Spirit.'

So, if people are being convinced of their need of Christ and led to him; if their belief that Christ appeared in history is strengthened; if they are more convinced than ever that he is the Son of God sent to save sinners; if they acknowledge that he is the only Saviour and they need him desperately; if they appreciate him more than they did, and love him too - we may be quite sure that it is the *Holy* Spirit who is at work! (Saying this, I do recognise that we may still not be able to determine whether his work and these convictions have yet *saved* the people involved. That is a different question.)

The precise words of the apostle are important. The Spirit gives testimony to the *true* Jesus who appeared in the flesh - not to some false, substitute Christ, such as the Christ of the old mystic or today's liberals. These people may praise their own, false Christ while having no respect at all for the true, historical Jesus. Indeed, they are led away from *him*. But no spirit can give testimony to the true Jesus, or lead men to him, except the Spirit of God.

Why is this the case? Because the devil has a bitter and unchanging hatred for the real Jesus, especially as Saviour. He passionately hates the story and the doctrine of redemption. Satan would never work in men to produce honourable thoughts of Jesus, nor cause them to value his commands. The Spirit that turns men's hearts to 'the seed of the woman' is not the spirit of the serpent that has such an unchanging hatred towards him. The Spirit that lifts men's appreciation of the glorious Michael, prince of angels, is not the spirit of the dragon that wars against him.

This then is the first sign that the Holy Spirit is at work. When we look at anything that is happening in the religious world, and need to pass judgement, the first question we must ask is: 'Are these people coming to love, honour and esteem the real Lord Jesus more than ever?'

2. When Satan's Kingdom is attacked

The Spirit of God must be at work if the interests of Satan's kingdom are opposed. This is a sure sign. Satan's kingdom encourages sin and encourages men to cherish worldly lusts; the Holy Spirit does not.

This sign is given in the fourth and fifth verses. 'You, dear children, are from God and have overcome them, because the one who is in you is greater than the one who is in the world.

37

They are from the world, and therefore speak from the viewpoint of the world, and the world listens to them.' The apostle is here comparing those that are influenced by two opposite kinds of spirits. One spirit is true, the other is false. John shows the difference like this: one spirit is from God and so *overcomes* the spirit of the world. The other spirit speaks about and *relishes* the things of the world. Here, the spirit of the devil is called 'the one who is in the world.' This is the difference between Christ and the devil; Christ says 'My kingdom is not of this world' but Satan is called 'the god of this world.'

We know what the apostle means by 'the world' or 'the things that are of the world' from his own words in chapter 2:15,16. 'Do not love the world or anything in the world. If anyone loves the world, the love of the Father is not in him. For everything in the world - the cravings of sinful man, the lust of his eyes and the boasting of what he has and does - comes not from the Father but from the world.' Plainly he means everything to do with sin and includes all men's corruptions and lusts, everything they look to for satisfaction.

So, from what the apostle says here we may safely conclude that if a people:

a) have their love of ordinary, worldly pleasure, profits and honours lowered
b) are weaned from eagerly chasing such things
c) have a deep concern about eternity and the eternal happiness that comes through the gospel
d) earnestly begin to seek God's kingdom and righteousness
e) are convicted of the ugliness and guilt of sin, as well as the misery to which it leads
   - then the Spirit of God must be at work.

We cannot believe that Satan would convict men of sin and awaken the conscience. The conscience is God's representative in the soul; it can do Satan no good to make its light shine brighter. It is always in his interest to keep the conscience quiet and asleep. When conscience is awake, with its eyes and mouth open, everything that Satan wants to accomplish is hindered. When he is out to lead men further into sin, would the devil first open their eyes to see its ugliness? Would he make them afraid of sin? Would he make them mourn over past sins? Would he show them that they need to be delivered from sin's guilt? Would he make them more careful about everything they do, to ensure there is no sin in it? Would the devil lead them to avoid future sins, and make them more careful to avoid his own temptations? If a man thinks the devil acts like this, I wonder what he uses for brains!

But some may argue that the devil may even awaken a man's conscience in order to deceive him - that is, to make him think he has been saved while he is still in his sin. To argue like this is futile. It is to argue that Christ was making a mistake when he told the Pharisees, 'Satan would not cast out Satan.' (Mt. 12:25,26) Remember, the Pharisees believed that the spirit at work in Christ's ministry was the devil. A man with an awakened conscience is the hardest man in the world to fool! The more awake a sinner's conscience is, the harder it is to quieten it down until it is really delivered from sin. The more a conscience is aware of the greatness of man's guilt, the less likely he is to be satisfied with his own righteousness. Once a man is thoroughly frightened by a sight of his own danger, he will not believe himself truly safe without good grounds. Awakening a conscience in this way is not likely to confirm a man in his sin; on the contrary, it is likely to lead to sin and Satan being driven out.

So, whenever we see people made aware of:

   a) the ugliness of sin
   b) God's anger against sin
   c) their own natural lostness because of sin
   d) their own need of eternal salvation
   e) their need of God's mercy and help
   f) their need to do what God has commanded in seeking salvation

we may certainly conclude that it is the Spirit of God at work!

Yes, even if their bodies are affected, and they cry out or scream or faint. Yes, even if they go into fits or are affected in other dramatic ways. *Those* things do not count at all.

3. When people come to love the Scriptures more

When men are persuaded to love the Holy Scriptures more, and trust their truth and divine origin more, it is certainly the Spirit of God at work. This is the sign the apostle gives us in the sixth verse: 'We are from God, and whoever knows God listens to us; but whoever is not from God does not listen to us. This is how we recognise the Spirit of truth and the spirit of false-hood.' When he says 'We are from God' he means 'We are the apostles God has sent to teach the world his doctrines and commands.' This argument extends to all those God has appointed to deliver to his church its rule of faith and practice. That is to say, it covers all those apostles and prophets that God has made the foundation of his church; in short, all those that he inspired to write the Scriptures.

The devil would never try to produce such a respect for God's Scriptures. A spirit of delusion will not persuade men to listen to God for direction. Evil spirits never cry 'To the law and to the testimony' (Is. 8:20) - that is God's way of exposing evil spirits and their teachings! The devil does not say, as Abraham did, 'They have Moses and the prophets; let them listen to them' (Lk. 16:29). Nor will he say the words that came from heaven about Christ, 'Listen to him' (Lk. 9:35).

Would the spirit of error, wanting to deceive men, turn them to God's infallible Scriptures? Would he lead them to get to know those Scriptures well? Would the prince of darkness lead men to the light of the Sun in order to promote his kingdom of darkness? The devil has always shown how much he hates the Bible; he has always done all he can to put out its light, and lead men away from it. He knows that this is the light which will overthrow his dark kingdom. He has had much experience of the power of Scripture to defeat his purposes and thwart his designs. It is a constant plague to him. It is the main weapon which Michael uses in his war with Satan; it is the sword of the Spirit, that pierces him and conquers him. It is that great and strong sword that God uses to punish Leviathan, the crooked serpent. It is the sharp sword that we read about (Rev. 19:15) that comes from the mouth of the one on the horse, with which he smites his enemies.

Every text of the Bible is a torment to the old serpent. He has felt its stinging smart thousands of times. He is therefore at war with the Bible, and hates every word in it. We may be quite sure he will never try to persuade men to love it or value it.

It has often happened in history that many sects of enthusiasts have undervalued the written word of God. They set up some other authority which is over the Scripture. That still happens today. But when men come to value the Scriptures more, not less, then the Spirit of God is certainly at work.

4. When men are led away from falsehood into truth.

We may learn another way to judge between spirits from the names given in verse six to the two opposite spirits. One is called 'the Spirit of truth' and the other 'the spirit of falsehood.'

These words point to a vital difference between the Spirit of God and other spirits that may imitate his work. If we see a spirit at work that is leading men into the truth, and convincing them of things that are true, we may be sure it is the Holy Spirit. For example, if people become more aware that there is a God, or that God is a great God who hates sin, or that their own lives are short and may end at any moment, or that there is another life and they have immortal souls - we may be sure it is the Holy Spirit at work. When men realise that they will have to give an account of themselves to God and that they are very sinful in nature and practice; when they understand that they are helpless in themselves to save themselves - when, in short, they are brought to sound doctrine - then we may be sure that the Holy

Spirit is at work in them.

It is the Holy Spirit who brings men into the light, not the spirit of darkness. Christ tells us that Satan is a liar and the father of lies; his kingdom is a kingdom of darkness. Satan's kingdom is upheld only by darkness and error; Scripture speaks of the reign and dominion of darkness. (Lk. 22:53, Col 1:13) The demons are called the rulers of the darkness of this world. It is only God who brings us to the light of truth and removes our darkness.

5. When there is an increase in love to God and man

When people begin to love God and man with a genuine love, we may be sure that the Holy Spirit is at work. This is what the apostle says next in the chapter we are looking at. 'Dear friends, let us love one another, for love comes from God. Everyone who loves has been born of God and knows God.' (verse 7) John is still speaking of two different sorts of people who are led by two opposite spirits, and pointing out the contrast between them. Love is one way we may know which person has the true spirit.

This is especially clear from verses 12 and 13. 'No-one has ever seen God; but if we love one another, God lives in us and his love is made complete in us. We know that we live in him and he in us, because he has given us of his Spirit.' Here, the apostle speaks of love and the Holy Spirit almost as if they are the same thing! If God's love dwells in us, he says, the Holy Spirit dwells in us. The same point is made in 3:22,23 and 4:16.

Love is the last sign the apostle gives us of the true Spirit's work and it seems to be the most important. He pays more attention to this than to all the rest. He tells us that love for God *and* love for our fellow men are both important. He writes of love for our fellow men in verses 7,11 and 12, and of love for God in verses 17,18 and 19. Then in verses 20 and 21 he speaks of both together, because he wants us to understand that love for men springs from love to God.

So if people have great thoughts of God and his glory, the Holy Spirit must be at work. If they understand (to some degree) the greatness of Jesus Christ so that they delight in him, the Holy Spirit must be at work. They may say that the Lord Jesus is 'the chief among ten thousand' and 'the altogether lovely one.' He becomes very precious to them and their hearts are overwhelmed by the wonderful and free love of God who gave his only Son to die for them. Surely this must be the Spirit of God at work! 'This is how God showed his love among us: he sent his one and only Son into the world that we might live through him. This is love: not that we loved God, but that he loved us and sent his Son as an atoning sacrifice for our sins. And we know and rely on the love God has for us. We love because he first loved us.' (verses 9,10,16,19)

If a spirit makes us love God for these reasons, it must be the Spirit of God. If we delight to think about the attributes of God that the gospel and Christ reveal, and long for fellowship with him and yearn to be made like him, living in ways that please and honour him - that must be the Spirit of God. When a spirit calms quarrels between men and promotes peace and goodwill and many acts of kindness and desires for the salvation of souls, this must be the Spirit of God. When men delight in the company of others who are obviously God's children, and have all the love I have described, we have the highest possible evidence that it is the Holy Spirit who is at work.

Yes, there is a counterfeit love which may appear among those led by a false and deluding spirit. Yet this is not the same thing at all as the true and Christian love which the apostle describes in this chapter. The wildest sort of fanatics often have a real union and bond of affection between them, but it is no more than evidence of self-love! They love one another because they agree about their peculiarities - those things which make everyone else ridicule them! So, for example, the ancient Gnostics and the fanatics that appeared at the time of the Reformation all boasted of their great love for one another.

One group even called themselves 'the family of love!' But this passage says enough about true Christian love to enable us to know the true from the false.

True love comes from understanding the wonderful riches of God's free and sovereign love to us in Christ. It is accompanied by a knowledge of our absolute unworthiness - see verses 9, 10, 11 and 19. True godly and supernatural love is distinguished from all counterfeits because the Christian virtue of humility shines in it. This true love is accompanied by a hatred and a renouncing of everything which we call 'self.' Christian love is a humble love. 'Love is patient, love is kind. It does not envy, it does not boast, it is not proud. It is not rude, it is not self-seeking.' (1 Cor 13:4,5)

So when we see love for one another coupled with a sense of personal unworthiness and poverty of spirit, it is a sure sign that the Spirit of God is at work. When a man has this love, God dwells in him. The love which John says is great evidence of the true Spirit is called God's love or Christ's love, vs. 12 ('his love is made complete in us'). We know what kind of love this is by Christ's example. His love was not only love to friends, but to enemies as well; and a love that was accompanied by a gentle and humble spirit. 'Learn from me' says the Lord Jesus, 'for I am gentle and humble in heart' (Mt. 11:29). Love and humility are the two things most different from the devils' nature; above everything else, he is full of pride and malice.

Conclusion
to the first two sections.

I have now explained the various marks the apostle gives us as signs that the Holy Spirit is at work.

There are some things the devil *would not* do if he could: he would not awaken the conscience and show men their need of a Saviour. He would not establish them in the belief that Jesus is the Son of God and the Saviour of sinners, or lead them to love him. He would not persuade men that the Scriptures are God's word and encourage them to study them diligently. He would not reveal to men the truth about their souls' need and bring them out of darkness into the light.

There are other things that the devil *cannot and will not* do. He will not give men a spirit of divine love or Christian humility or poverty of spirit; he could not do it even if he wanted to. He cannot give to others what he does not possess himself; these things are foreign to his nature.

So we can conclude then like this: when there is a powerful influence on the minds of people we are safe in concluding that the Holy Spirit is at work if these things are found. This is true whatever other things may be present, whatever people are the instruments involved, whatever means are being used (for God is sovereign and we cannot understand all he does) and whatever effects may be visible in men's bodies. These marks that the apostle has given are sufficient to stand alone and support themselves. They plainly show the finger of God and are quite enough to outweigh a thousand little objections that may come from oddities, irregularities and errors in conduct - or, for that matter, the delusions and scandals of some who claim to have been affected.

But *are* these marks sufficient?

Some would say that these marks are not sufficient, and point to Paul's words in 2 Corinthians: 'Such men are false apostles, deceitful workmen, masquerading as apostles of Christ. And no wonder, for Satan himself masquerades as an angel of light.' (11:13,14) They argue that Paul is here saying it is impossible to make any judgement, given that Satan can masquerade like this.

But that is not what the apostle is saying. These false prophets whom John mentions are the same sort as the false apostles whom Paul mentions, in whom the devil masqueraded as an angel of light. John is quite deliberately telling us how to distinguish the true from the false *in spite of* the masquerade! When he says 'Do not believe every spirit, but test the spirits to see whether they are from God' and gives as his reason that many false prophets have gone out into the world, he is saying 'Many have gone out into the world who are the ministers of the devil, though they claim to be prophets of God. In them, the devil is masquerading as an angel of light. Use these rules I am giving you so that you can tell the true from the false.'

If we examine the New Testament to see what else is said about these false prophets and false apostles, we will not find anything to contradict this. For example, the devil is masquerading as an angel of light when there are great boasts of extraordinary knowledge - Col 2:8, 1 Tim 1:6,7, 6:3-5; 2 Tim 2:14-18, Titus 1:10, 16. In the early days of the church, followers of these men called themselves 'Gnostics' from their claim to have special knowledge. The devil in them also mimicked the miraculous gifts of the Holy Spirit, with visions, revelations, prophecies and so on. So these men were called false apostles and false prophets: see Mt. 24:24. Again there was a false claim to great holiness and spiritual talk: Rom 16:17,18, Eph. 4:14. So they are called deceitful workers, and wells and clouds without water, 2 Cor 11:13, 2 Peter 2:17, Jude 12. Fourthly there were elements of superstitious worship

46

which they claimed showed them to be more holy, Col. 2:16-23. As a result, they had a false and bitter zeal, Gal 4:17, 18, 1 Tim 1:6 and 6:4,5. Fifthly there was an outward show of humility when they were, in fact, far from humble. (Col 2:18,23) But does any of this affect what has been said about the true marks of the Spirit? Not at all!

I have done what I set out to do - that is, show how we may be sure whether God is at work or not. Now I will proceed to apply what I have said.

Section 3:

Some practical inferences

1: This revival is genuine

My first inference is this: from what has been said, it is impossible to deny that the revival which has lately appeared is, in general, from the Holy Spirit.

In order to make a judgement on any matter, we need to know only two things. We need to know what the facts are, and what the rules for making a judgement are. In a case like this, the rules are those that the Word of God contains and which I have expounded above. We have spent a long time looking at the rules, so we need now to turn to the facts and ask: what is actually happening in this great revival in New England? There are only two ways we can know what is going on. One is to see for ourselves; the other is to take the information from those who have seen for themselves.

In this revival the facts are so clear that we must conclude that God is at work, or else conclude that the rules for judging that John gives are wrong! For example, in this revival many people are turning their attentions away from the emptiness of the world. They are concerned instead - and very deeply concerned - about eternal happiness. They seek their salvation earnestly; they have been thoroughly convinced of their sin and guilt. Their consciences are awakened; they are aware of the dreadfulness of God's anger and have begun to seek his grace. They are far more zealous to use properly the ways God has given for us to know him. They are particularly earnest about the Word of God; they love to read it and to hear it, and to know it better than they did.

The Holy Spirit is the Spirit of truth, and it is well known that those who are affected by this revival have a greater understanding of the truth. People are more aware than ever of what really is true in eternal things: that they must die, that life is short and uncertain; that there is a great God who hates sin and to whom they must give account; that he will judge them eternally; that they are in great need of a Saviour. It makes them more aware of the preciousness of that Jesus who was crucified, and more aware too of their great need of him. As a result of this, they seek him earnestly.

These things must be well known throughout the land, for they were not done 'in a corner.' This revival has not been confined to a few towns in remote places, but has been at work in many places all over the land - especially in the largest and most well-populated areas. In this respect Christ has performed his miracles among us just as he did in Judea. This revival has been going on for a considerable time, so there has been plenty of opportunity to observe and to reflect on what is happening. Everyone who knows those involved sees a great deal that, according to the rules John gives, show this revival to be God at work.

Are we deceived (or deceiving others)?

This question is much easier to answer when a revival has been carried on amongst a great many people in many different places. If only a few people were involved, we could reasonably suspect deception. A few people may pretend, and claim things that have never happened to them and experiences they have never known. But when the work is spread over a great part of the country, and people of all sorts and ages; when many sane and sensible people are affected who have been well educated and whose integrity is well known, then it is absurd to suggest that we cannot make any real judgement about what is happening! The revival has been going on for months. Those who know the people involved well are quite capable of judging whether those people have been spiritually awakened or not. Similarly, they can judge whether they love the Scriptures more or less, as well as whether they are more concerned with their salvation than they were before, or less.

Some people object though because this seems like fanaticism to them. It is not so easy, they say, to tell whether people have been saved as they think I am suggesting! Let us grant that for a moment; but an important distinction needs to be made. It *may* be presumptuous or arrogant to say that we believe certain truths and have been saved by them. But it cannot be presumptuous or arrogant to say that we are more convinced about those truths than we used to be! If anyone wants to quibble with the first statement because of the strong assurance of salvation that it implies, they still have no right to quibble with the second statement. Honest and sensible people may expect their word to be believed in this matter! In fact, even with the first statement, many people are less likely to be mistaken than a few.

But whether the effect on people's minds and hearts have led to their salvation is beside the point for the moment. If their love for Christ and the Scriptures have been increased in the way described, then it is a sure sign that the Spirit of God has been at work. The rules of the Scriptures apply equally well whether the object of the Spirit's work is saved or not.

Causes of offence in this revival
By God's providence I have for some months past spent much time with those people who have been the subjects of this revival. In particular, I have had many opportunities to see those things which are causing most offence to some - that is, people crying out, loud shrieking and so on. I have seen both what has happened, *and* the fruit of what has happened, over a period of several months. Some of the people affected I know very well, and have been their pastor both before and since they were affected. For this reason I regard it as my duty to give my

testimony that, as far as it is humanly possible to tell, this revival has all the marks that I have pointed out from John's epistle. In many people, it is true that every single one of the marks indicated is present; and in very many, it is true that they are all present to a very great degree.

The people involved in those things that have given so much offence have usually been affected in one of two ways. Some have suffered great distress when they have seen their own sin; others have been overcome with a sense of the greatness and wonder and excellency of divine things. Let me speak of each group individually.

The first group: those distressed by their own sin.
In these cases, distress has almost always arisen from a real conviction of the truth about themselves There have been very few people who appeared to be faking their distress in any degree; there have been very many who were quite unable to control it. They have not taken leave of their senses; those who were able to speak during their distress have been well able to explain what was happening and why they were so distressed at the time. Afterwards, too, they have been able to remember what had happened and why. I have known a very few people who, in their extreme distress, seem for a short time to have lost their reason to some degree; but although I have seen hundreds, maybe thousands, that have recently experienced such distress of soul I have not known a single one to have lost their reason permanently.

It is true that I have known some cases where depression in a medical sense seems to have been mixed with conviction of sin; when that happens the difference is quite clear. These people are not only distressed by the truth, but empty shadows and strange ideas distress them and cannot be dealt with either by Scripture or reason.

Some people, while appearing to me to be under genuine conviction of sin and distressed as a result, have not been able to explain very well what has been happening to them. Yet the end result in their cases has still been good. Of course, none of this will surprise those who have any experience of dealing with souls under spiritual difficulty. The experiences of such people are completely new to them and they do not know how to express themselves. Some who at first did not know how to express themselves or what to say have, on further examination, been well able to explain their condition.

Some suppose that the great convictions I have described are produced by nothing more than ordinary, human fear. But we need to make a careful distinction between the fear or distress which is produced by an awareness of some awesome truth (a fear that may be fully justified by the truth itself) and a fear or distress which has no real cause.

This last sort of fear is of one of two kinds. First, it may be that people are terrified by something which is not true. I have seen very little of this, except in cases of depression. But secondly, others may be frightened by some outward thing which they see or hear without knowing what it is. They are afraid it is something terrible, but their minds are not being affected by any particular truth at all. Again, I have seen very little of this at all, either with the young or old people involved in this current revival. On the contrary, those who are most terrified under this revival are well able to explain why. They speak of feeling their own very great wickedness and their very many sins. They speak of how polluted their hearts are, and how much they have hated God and loved all that is evil. They are aware of how stubborn they have been, and how hard their hearts are; they tell of their great sense of guilt before God and the dreadful punishment that all sin deserves. Very often they have clear and vivid ideas of eternal punishment in hell; at the same time, they know that God has them in his hands and is very angry against sin. The greatness of his wrath is dreadful to them. They believe they have provoked God so much that his anger is ready to overflow; they are in great danger, they believe, for God will not be patient with them any longer. Even now he is ready to end their lives and send them down to that hell they can see so clearly - and they can see no hope for themselves. More and more they realise how vain and empty their previous hopes have been; they have trusted in things which can never save them. Now they are at the mercy of God, but he is angry. Very many have seen quite clearly that they fully deserve his wrath and the hell that they can almost feel. While they fear every moment that hell will open before them, yet they feel too that it would be no more than they deserve, and they know that God is indeed Lord, and able to do as he wants. I need hardly point out that all these things are true and Scriptural - and a fear that comes from understanding these things is perfectly reasonable!

Very often these people have been calmed by some text of Scripture which speaks of God's sovereignty; such texts have helped them to trust him. After great agonies of soul, they have been able to submit to the will of a just and sovereign God, even before they have seen the light of the gospel. At these times they may be without much bodily strength, and it seem that their lives were almost at an end - and then God's light has shone in their darkness. The glorious Redeemer, with his wonderful grace sufficient even for them, has made himself known to them from some passage of the Scripture. Sometimes that light has entered their heart suddenly, sometimes more gradually. But it still fills their souls with love, admiration, joy and humility. They have begun to love this excellent Redeemer and longed just to humble themselves before him. They have longed too that others might see him, embrace him and be delivered by him. They have longed to live to his glory, yet know that they can do nothing by themselves; they see themselves as very sinful, and are very suspicious of their own hearts.

As time goes on with such people it becomes even more clear that there has been a real change of heart, and following this God's grace has acted just as it does in those converted outside of revival. They experience the same difficulties and temptations and trials and comforts. The main difference, though, is this: that very often the light they have enjoyed and the comforts they have experienced have been to a much greater degree than normal. Many very young children have had just these experiences. There have been some cases very much like those we read of in Mark 1:26 and 9:26, where we read 'The evil spirit shook the man violently and came out of him with a shriek.' (Perhaps these Scriptures are there to prepare us for cases like this.) Some have been through such agonies several times before being delivered; sadly, others have had the same distresses which have passed away without salvation resulting.

Is this a great confusion?

Some object that all this is a great confusion - many people together making a great noise. Therefore God cannot be behind it, they say, for he is the God of order, not of confusion. But they have not understood what 'confusion' is! Confusion occurs when what we are doing is interrupted so that its object and purpose is *not* achieved. But the object and purpose of our gathering together for public worship is that sinners should be convicted and converted. I do believe that those who can restrain themselves and not make any noise, should do so; but if God arranges it so that many cannot stop themselves, I do not believe that this is 'confusion' any more than it would be if we were meeting in a field and our worship was stopped by a downpour! May God grant that all our services be broken off like this next Sunday! We should not be sorry that our services are interrupted, if their purpose - conviction and conversion - is achieved by that interruption! A man who is going to fetch a treasure does not feel cheated if he meets that treasure half way!

The second group: those overcome with a sense of the greatness of God

Now let me speak briefly of those in the second group. Besides those who are overcome with conviction of sin and fear of punishment, I have seen many lately who have lost all their bodily strength by a sense of the glorious excellency of the Redeemer, and the wonders of his dying love. This has been accompanied by a very unusual sense of their own littleness and vileness, and expressions of great humility and self-hatred.

This has not only happened to new converts. Many who, we trust, were converted previously have known much joy and love, accompanied by many tears. They have been very contrite and humble that they have not lived more to God's glory than they have. They have seen their own vileness more clearly, and the evil of their own hearts. They have been very earnest to live better lives in future, yet are more aware of their own inability than ever. Many have been overcome with pity for others, and longing for their salvation.

There are many other things, too, that I might mention from this astonishing revival, which fit in with every one of those marks I have insisted on. If the apostle John knew how to give the signs of a true work of the Spirit, then this is such a work!

Comparison with past revivals.
Providence has placed me in a town where God has worked in revival before. For two years I had the happiness of working in this town with the old and much-respected Stoddard. At that time I knew a good number who were affected by revivals during his ministry. Their experiences were consistent with the doctrine of all orthodox theologians; and it is generally accepted by respected ministers that those revivals were genuine. This new revival has affected the same town (as well as others) and I can testify that it is plainly the same kind of work as the previous ones, even though the circumstances are different. If this is not, in general, God at work then we need to throw away our Bibles, give up revealed religion and abandon all talk of conversion and Christian experience.

The faults of this revival
What of the faults in this revival? There have been occasions where people have not acted wisely. There have also been

irregularities and some delusion, as many have noticed.

But is that surprising, after such a long period of deadness? It is almost inevitable that there should be problems in the early days. When God first created the world, he did not make it perfect at once. There was a great deal of imperfection, darkness and even chaos and confusion *after* God first said 'Let there be light.' Then, when God first began to deliver his people from their long bondage in Egypt, there were false miracles mixed with the true for a while, and as a result the Egyptians became hard and doubted that God was really at work. When the children of Israel first went to fetch back the ark of God, after they had neglected it and it had been absent a long time, they did not do everything as they ought to have done. (1 Chron. 15:13.) When the sons of God came to present themselves before the Lord, Satan came as well with them. When Solomon's ships brought gold silver and pearls, they also brought apes and peacocks. When daylight first appears after a night of darkness, we must expect to have darkness and light mixed together for a while, not to have the sun risen at once to its noon-day splendour! As fruit is first green before it is ripe, and comes to its proper perfection only gradually, so it is with the kingdom of God, as Christ tells us. (Mk. 4:26-29)

The examples of lack of wisdom and errors are even less surprising when we remember that it is mostly young people who have been affected by this revival. Naturally they have less experience and, having all the energy of youth, are more liable to run to extremes. Satan will keep men bound as long as he can; but when he can hold them no longer he will try and drive them to extremes. In this way he hopes to dishonour God and damage true religion.

I firmly believe that one reason there has been so much error is that in many places people can see that their ministers do not approve of what is happening. They therefore dare not ask guidance of their ministers (who are appointed to guide them) and so are without guides. It is not surprising then that when people are like sheep without a shepherd they wander off the path! People in such circumstances have great and continual need of guides, and the guides themselves have great need of more wisdom than they naturally possess.

Even where a congregation has ministers that approve of the revival and rejoice in it, yet we should not expect either ministers or people to know exactly what to do in such extraordinary circumstances. It is new, and they need time and experience to learn how to judge the various things that are happening. We have experience of this among my own people. This current revival is much purer than the one we experienced six years ago; it has seemed more purely spiritual, more free from corruption and only spoiled by a little extravagance. It has produced a more thorough humiliation before God and men. The difference has been remarkable in one respect especially; while previously the height of their joy and the depth of their experiences made them forget how much greater God is than they are, so that they spoke with too much lightness of their own experiences, now there seems to be no tendency that way. On the contrary, their rejoicing is a more solemn rejoicing, and more reverential, as God commands. (Ps. 2:11) This is not because the joy is not as great; in many cases it is much greater. Many among us who were much affected in that previous revival have had even greater heavenly experiences than they had then. But their rejoicing humbles them; it breaks their hearts and levels them to the dust. When they speak of their joys, it is not with laughter but with floods of tears. Those that laughed before, now weep; and yet they would all agree that their joy is greater and purer and sweeter than it was before. They are now more like Jacob who, when God appeared to him at Bethel, said 'How awesome is this place.' They are like Moses who, when God revealed his glory, bowed to the ground and worshipped.

2: We must not hinder this genuine revival

My second inference is this: let us be warned to do nothing that will hinder this revival in any way; on the contrary, we must do our utmost to promote it. Christ's power is being shown in a remarkable and wonderful work of his Spirit; all his disciples must acknowledge him, and give him the honour he deserves.

God's work is not always recognised by those who claim to be believers. The example of the Jews in the time of the Lord Jesus and his apostles is enough to prove this. Those who do not acknowledge that this revival is genuine need to be very cautious. When Christ was in the world, the world did not know him. He came to those who claimed to be his people, but they did not receive him. That coming of Christ was prophesied much in the Scriptures and it had been long expected. Yet, because Christ came in a way that they did not expect, and which did not suit their own worldly reason, they would not acknowledge him. Instead they opposed him, they called him a madman and declared that he produced his miracles not by the Spirit of God but by the spirit of the devil. They were amazed at the great things he did, and did not know what to make of them; but they would not acknowledge him.

Those same Jews would not believe when the Spirit of God was poured out so wonderfully in the apostles' days. They regarded it as a false work. They were astonished by what they saw, but they were not convinced. Those who rejected the work most forcefully were those who were most sure of their own wisdom. (The Scriptures speak of this: 'Therefore once more will I astound these people with wonder upon wonder; the wisdom of the wise will perish, the intelligence of the intelligent will vanish.' Is. 29:14) Many people who had a great reputation for their religion and holiness despised what God was doing. Why? Because they could see that it demolished their standing and honour, and rebuked their religion which was merely formal and lukewarm. For these reasons some openly opposed the work of the Spirit of God and called it the work of the devil. This was contrary to their own consciences, and so they were guilty of the unpardonable sin against the Holy Spirit. Those who do not acknowledge that this revival is genuine must be careful in all that they say and do!

Scriptural prophecy also speaks of another, spiritual, coming of Christ to set up his kingdom in the world. This too has been long expected by God's church. The Bible leads us to believe that it will, in many respects, be like our Lord's first coming. It is certainly true that the low state of the church now is very like the state of the Jewish church when Christ came. So it is not a surprise that this revival appears strange to most people. In fact, it would be a great surprise if this were not the case!

Whether or not this current revival is the beginning of Christ setting up his kingdom, it is clear from all I have said that the same Spirit is at work and in the same kind of way. We may be sure that those who continue to oppose the revival and refuse to acknowledge that Christ is at work will bring down the displeasure of God, just as those Jews did who refused to acknowledge Christ. This is especially true of those who are teachers in his church. It will not do for them to argue that there are stumbling-blocks in the way, and that there are real reasons to doubt the work. The teachers of the Jewish church found innumerable stumbling-blocks, and regarded them as insurmountable. Many things about Christ, and about the work of his Spirit after the ascension, seemed strange to them; they were sure that they had good reasons for their objections. Christ and his work were, to the Jews, a stumbling-block; but Christ said 'Blessed is the man who does not fall away on account of me.' (Mt. 11:6) Despite all their reasons, Christ had not been at work long in Judea before those who refused to acknowledge him brought great guilt on themselves in God's sight. So Christ condemned them, saying that although they could 'interpret the appearance of the earth and the sky' yet they could not interpret the present times; he asked 'Why don't you judge for yourselves what is right?' (Lk. 11:54-57)

In our day the great Jehovah has come among us in mighty power. He has done many remarkable things. Those who refuse to admit his presence will be guilty! The Lord has appeared in such a glorious work of power and grace. He has appeared in such public places almost throughout the land, and given much evidence of his presence. Yet many do not receive him or acknowledge him; they do not appear to rejoice in his gracious presence or even to thank him once for such blessings. To be silent here must surely provoke God to anger, when he has done so much! Yes, even to be silent is to oppose the work and to do so silently, secretly. Such ministers are standing in the way of God's work, as Christ said 'He who is not with me is against me.' (Mt. 12:30)

Those who are still wondering what to make of this revival, and especially those who speak contemptuously of it, need to think about Paul's words to those Jews who were in the same position: 'Take care that what the prophets have said does not happen to you: "Look you scoffers, wonder and perish, for I am going to do something in your days that you would never believe, even if someone told you."' (Acts 13:40,41) Surely they ought to tremble at these words! Those who think the work cannot be true just because it is so powerful and extensive should think about the unbelieving soldier in Samaria, who said 'Even if the Lord should open the floodgates of the heavens, could this happen?' (2 Kings 7:2) Elisha said to him 'You will see it with your own eyes, but you will not eat any of it.' The pillar of cloud and fire was a pillar of darkness to the Egyptians; if this revival is a pillar of darkness to you, beware that it does not lead to your destruction, even while it is giving light to God's church!

Some are content simply to wait, and comfort themselves by the thought that they are being prudent, waiting to see what happens. They want to see what fruit those involved in the revival will bear. I earnestly ask these people to consider whether such 'prudence' justifies refusing to recognise Christ who is so wonderfully and graciously present in this land. They may be waiting for fruit, but they do not know what they are waiting for. They are quite incapable of recognising fruit when it comes! If they wait to see a work of God that is perfect and without any problems, they are like a fool waiting at the river side until all the water has run by. A work of God without stumbling-blocks is never to be expected. 'Such things must come.' (Mt. 18:7) God has never sent a revival yet without there being many problems associated with it. It is the same with God's works as it is with his word: at first, it seems full of difficult, strange and inconsistent things. Christ and his work always was and always will be a stone that causes men to stumble. The prophet Hosea (chapter 14) speaks of a glorious revival of religion in God's church. He speaks of a revival when God would be like the dew to Israel, a revival whose branches should spread and then concludes: 'Who is wise? He will realise these things. Who is discerning? He will understand them. The ways of the Lord are right; the righteous walk in them, but the rebellious stumble in them.'

Those who are 'waiting to see what happens' think that, given time, they will be able to make a better judgement. I doubt it. It may well be that the stumbling-blocks associated with this revival will increase, and not diminish. It is likely that we shall see more cases of apostasy and great sin among those who have been affected. If one kind of stumbling-block is removed, no doubt others will come. Christ's works are like his parables: the difficult things are there deliberately. God has put them there to test our spiritual sense, so that those who are of an unbelieving, perverse and complaining spirit 'though seeing they may not see.' (Lk. 8:10) The Jews that saw Christ's miracles waited to see better proof that he was the Messiah; they wanted a sign from heaven. They waited in vain. Their stumbling-blocks did not diminish, but they increased. There was no end to them, and their unbelief became stronger and stronger. Many people who have been praying for that glorious revival which Scripture speaks of did not know what they were praying for. (Again, this is just like the Jews when they prayed for the coming of Christ.) If God sent that revival in their day, they would not admit it or recognise it.

Those who claim to be being most *careful* will probably turn out to have been most *careless*. By waiting so long before they admit that God is at work, they will fail to share in this great blessing. They will miss the most precious opportunity of obtaining divine light, grace and comfort that God ever gave to New England. The glorious fountain is open, and multitudes flock to it and are satisfied. Yet these others wait so long in the distance, that they will soon have waited until the fountain is closed! It is astonishing that those who have had their doubts about this work have not done more investigating. If they had gone to the places where the revival is at its most powerful; if they had investigated the people most clearly affected (not one or two, but many) - then surely they would have been convinced.

Many have made a great mistake, criticising the revival on the basis of hearsay alone! They would have been better to follow the example of unbelieving Gamaliel: 'Leave these men alone! Let them go! For if their purpose or activity is of human origin, it will fail. But if it is from God, you will not be able to stop these men; you will only find yourselves fighting against God.' (Acts 5:38,39) I do not know whether I have said enough here to convince these doubters, or not; but I hope that in the future they will at least learn from Gamaliel's caution. If they do, they will not oppose the revival, or say anything which might discredit it indirectly, to ensure that they do not oppose the Holy Spirit. It would be better to speak against God the Father, or God the Son, than to speak against the Holy Ghost and his work in the hearts of men. Nothing is so likely to stop us ever receiving any benefit from him in our own souls!

If some still go on determined to speak evil of these things, I beg them to be careful that they do not become guilty of the unpardonable sin. Surely it is at a time like this, when the Holy Spirit is among us and working powerfully, that this sin is most likely. If this revival continues, it will be very surprising if some of its opponents do not become guilty of this sin. In fact, they may be guilty already. Those who maliciously oppose this revival and say that it is the work of the devil are only one step away from the unpardonable sin. That step is this: that they should oppose it against their own consciences and inner convictions. And while some are being very careful not to oppose or criticise this work openly, yet I am afraid that at a time like this many who are silent (especially ministers) will bring that curse of the angel of the Lord upon themselves. "'Curse Meroz,' said the angel of the Lord. 'Curse its people bitterly, because they did not come to help the Lord, to help the Lord against the mighty.'" (Judges 5:23)

Since the great God has shown himself so wonderfully in this land we must expect everybody to be affected by it one way or the other. Those who do not benefit from it spiritually will surely become more guilty and miserable. It is always like that; if it is an acceptable year and a time of great favour to those who accept it, it is a day of vengeance to the others. (Is. 59:2) When God sends out his word it does not return to him empty; much less his Spirit. When Christ was upon earth in Judea, many rejected him; yet they were not allowed to escape the consequences of that. God made all the people know that Christ had been among them; those who did not benefit by it, sorrowed by it. When God sent the prophet Ezekiel to the children of Israel, he declared that whether they listened to him or not they would know that a prophet had been among them. We may be sure that God will make everyone know that Jehovah has been in New England!

3: Let the revival's friends be careful

My third and final inference must be applied to those who are the friends of this revival, who have benefited from it and are keen to promote it. Let me earnestly exhort you all to be very careful. Avoid all errors and misconduct, and anything else that will obscure the brightness of the revival. Give no opportunity at all to those who are just looking for an excuse to criticise. The apostle encourages Titus to take great care with both his preaching and his behaviour: Titus 2:7,8. We need to be as wise as serpents and as harmless as doves. In days of blessing like this, it is very important that we behave in an innocent and wise manner. We must expect that Satan, the great enemy of this revival, will try his hardest to mislead us. It will be a great victory for him if he succeeds. He knows that it will do more to further his cause than if he had victories over a hundred others. We need to watch and pray, for we are only little children; the roaring lion is too strong for us, and the old serpent too subtle for us.

Humility and an entire dependence on our Lord Jesus Christ will be our best defence. Let us therefore take great care not to become spiritually proud. Let us be careful that we do not become boastful about the extraordinary blessings and experiences that we might have received. After such blessings we need to take particular care with our own hearts, so that we do not begin to think of ourselves as among the best of God's people. We must not assume that we are the ones most able to instruct and reprove this evil generation. We must not think that we are prophets or extraordinary ambassadors of heaven. When we have remarkable experiences of God, we must not become conceited. Moses, when he had been speaking with God in the mountain, had a shining face which dazzled Aaron and the people; yet Moses himself could not see it. (Ex. 34:23)

Pride is a danger for all of us; God saw that even Paul was in danger of it. Though Paul was, perhaps. the greatest saint who ever lived; and though he had spoken with God in the third heaven (2 Cor 12:7) - yet still he was in danger of pride. Pride is the heart's worst snake; it is the first sin that ever entered the universe. It is the lowest foundation of the whole building of sin, and is the most secret and deceitful of all the sins. It is ready to mix with everything. Nothing is so hateful to God; nothing is so contrary to the whole spirit of the gospel. Nothing harms the gospel as much as pride. There is no sin that does as much to give the devil entry into the hearts of the saints as pride. I have seen it happen many times, and with great saints. The devil has attacked them in this way immediately after some great experience, and has led the saint astray. Only God can then open the eyes and allow them to see that it was pride that betrayed them.

To help as much as I can, I want to give some specific areas where I believe the friends of the revival need to be careful:

A. Do not put too much confidence in strong impressions on the mind. Some of those who have been true friends of the revival have made this mistake. They have been too ready to follow impulses and strong impressions on the mind. They have acted as though they have had direct revelations from heaven about the mind of God, about matters where the Bible says nothing. This is to claim far more than the Spirit's gracious influence in our hearts; it is to claim the gifts of the Spirit, and true inspiration of the same kind as the prophets and apostles. The apostle distinguishes these from the *grace* of the Spirit - 1 Cor. 13.

One reason why some people have been ready to give too much importance to these impressions is a wrong opinion they have held about the coming millennium. They have believed that the glory of that age would consist partly in the supernatural gifts of the Spirit being restored to the church. They hold this view, I believe, because they have not properly considered either the nature or the value of the two different influences of the Spirit. He works in two ways in the believer - one is 'ordinary' and gracious, the other is extraordinary and miraculous.

The apostle shows in the passage beginning at 1 Cor 12:31 that it is the ordinary, gracious gifts that are the best and most glorious. When he speaks of the supernatural gifts of the Spirit he says 'eagerly desire the greater gifts. And now I will show you the most excellent way.' (That is, the most excellent way the Spirit influences us.) Then he goes on, in the next chapter, to show that the most excellent way is the gift of divine love. Throughout that chapter he shows how much more we should prefer love to inspiration. God communicates his own nature to the soul far more by giving saving grace to the heart than by miraculous gifts. It is grace, not gifts, that reveal the image of God. The soul is most happy and glorious when it has the graces, not the gifts. Grace is a tree which bears infinitely better fruit. It is not those who have excellent gifts that are promised salvation and the eternal enjoyment of God, but those who have divine grace. In fact, a man may have supernatural gifts and still be abominable to God and go to hell.

True spirituality and eternal life in the soul consists in the grace of the Spirit; this God gives only to his favourites, his own dear children. Sometimes he has 'thrown out' the gifts to dogs and swine, as he did to Balaam, Saul and Judas. Some in the early church had these supernatural gifts who then committed the unforgivable sin, as Hebrews 6:4-6 shows. Many wicked men at the day of judgement will plead 'Did we not prophesy in your name, and in your name drive out demons and perform many miracles?' The greatest privilege of the apostles and prophets was not that they were inspired and worked miracles, but that they were holy. The grace in their hearts dignified them a thousand times more than their miraculous gifts.

David rejoices not because he is a King or a prophet but that the Spirit of God influences his heart in a holy manner, and reveals to him divine light and love and joy. The apostle Paul had many visions, as well as revelations and miraculous gifts. He had more of these than the other apostles, but still counts all things loss for the excellency of the spiritual knowledge of Christ. Christ directs the apostles to rejoice that their names are written in heaven, not that the devils are subject to them. Evidence that their names are written in heaven came not from their gifts, but their graces. To have grace in the heart is a greater privilege than the Virgin Mary had when the body of the second person of the Trinity was conceived in her womb by the Holy Spirit. (Lk 11:27,28. See also Mt. 12:47-50) To be influenced by the Spirit and have divine love in the heart is the greatest privilege and glory of the highest archangel in heaven; this is the very thing by which mere creatures may have fellowship with God himself, Father and Son, in their beauty and happiness. By this the saints are made partakers of the divine nature, and have Christ's joy fulfilled in themselves.

The ordinary, sanctifying work of the Spirit is the purpose for which all the miraculous gifts are given, as the apostle shows in Eph. 4:11,12,13. They are not good for anything unless they achieve this purpose; in fact not only will they not be good for any who are not made holy by them, they will add to their misery. This, the apostle says, is the most excellent way God communicates his Spirit to the church in all ages; it is the church's greatest glory. This glory is what makes the church on earth most like the church in heaven; for in heaven, of course, prophecy, tongues and all the miraculous gifts cease. In heaven God only gives his Spirit in that excellent way - charity or divine love - 'which never fails.'

So the glory of the approaching millennium does not require these supernatural gifts. In that day the church will be most like the perfect church in heaven, and I believe it will be like that church in this matter also: the supernatural gifts will have vanished away. They will be like the light of the stars and the moon, which are swallowed up in the sun of divine love. The apostle speaks of these gifts as childish things by comparison with the influence of the Spirit in bringing divine love. They are things given to the church only to help it through childhood. When the church has a full rule given, and all the ordinary means of grace are settled, they would cease as the church progressed to maturity and manhood. 1 Cor 13:11 says 'When I was a child, I talked like a child, I thought like a child, I reasoned like a child. When I became a man, I put childish ways behind me' - that is, the childish ways he speaks of in the previous three verses.

Some may think that the apostle is talking about heaven when he says that prophecies, tongues and revelations will stop and vanish from the church when it reaches maturity. But this cannot be. He is thinking of the church reaching a mature state in this world, because he speaks of a maturity where the gifts have ceased but faith, hope and love remain. He is drawing a contrast between what remains, and those things that fail, cease and pass away. (Vs. 8) The miraculous gifts cease, but faith, hope and love will remain. Therefore it must be the church on earth he is speaking of, and especially in the latter ages of the world. The church at Corinth needed to hear this for two main reasons: first, because he had already told them that they were in a state of infancy, (3:2), and second because that church, more than all others, seemed to abound with miraculous gifts. But when the glorious Millennium of the church comes, the increase of light shall be so great that it can be spoken of as seeing 'face to face' (vs. 12). See also Is. 24:23 and 35:7.

So I do not expect the miraculous gifts to be restored as the church's glorious days approach; and I do not want them to be restored. It seems to me that they would not make those days more glorious, but less so. It is much better to enjoy the sweet influences of the Spirit for one quarter of an hour than to have prophetic visions and revelations all year. These influences reveal Christ's spiritual divine beauty, his infinite grace and his dying love. They produce in the soul faith, love, sweet satisfaction and joy in God. Such immediate revelations were necessary in the early days of the church. They are not necessary now, as the most glorious and perfect state of the church on earth approaches. There is no need of these supernatural gifts to set up the kingdom of God throughout the world. In fact, I have seen so much of the power of God working in 'the most excellent way,' that I am convinced God can easily do without these things.

I would therefore most seriously ask God's people to be very careful how much attention they give to such things. I have seen prophecies and the like fail in many instances. I know by experience that although an impression may be made on the mind very powerfully, (even on the minds of great saints, and even in the midst of a time of great spiritual power and fellowship with God and, yes, even if they are accompanied by texts of Scripture,) it is no sure sign that it is a revelation from heaven. I have known such impressions be proved false, even though all the circumstances I have mentioned have been fulfilled. God has given us the Scriptures as a light shining in a dark place. Those who leave this sure word of prophecy to follow such impressions have left the guidance of the pole star to follow a wandering light. It is not surprising therefore that they are sometimes led into sad extremes.

B. Let us not neglect human learning and study. This really follows from the first; since we cannot expect direct revelation, let us not despise human learning. Those who say that human learning is of little or no use in the work of the ministry have not thought about what they are saying; if they had, they would not say it. Let them think about it now: to say that human learning is of no use is to say that educating a child is no use, or that the knowledge which adults have more than children is no use. If that were true, a child of four years old would be as capable a teacher in God's church as a well-instructed man of thirty - providing they both have the same grace. It would mean that they could both do as much to advance God's kingdom. But if we admit that adults do have greater abilities, and are able to accomplish more than children - well then, it follows that if their learning increases more, they will be able to do still more good. (Provided of course that their grace remains the same.) Of course, the more knowledge we have the more we are able to do, whether for good or ill, as we choose. It is too obvious for anyone to deny it that God made great use of human learning in the apostle Paul, and that he did so too in the cases of Moses and Solomon.

Then too if knowledge, obtained the ordinary way, is not to be despised, it naturally follows that the means of obtaining knowledge, that is study, is not to be neglected. Study is a great help for preparing to instruct others. Though some men, with their hearts full of the Spirit of God, have been able to speak very profitably without study, this does not justify others refusing study. That is like casting ourselves down from the pinnacle of the temple and trusting the angel of the Lord to catch us, when there is another, slower, way down! It does help too for preachers to take care with their presentation; well-ordered sermons are a help to both the understanding and the memory.

C. Let us beware of judging others. Another thing that Christians need to consider very carefully is the matter of judging others. Do the Scriptures give us the right to declare that others, who claim to be Christians, are hypocrites and not truly converted? If they do, on what grounds? We are often warned about judging others in Scripture, so we need to look very carefully at the rules we are given and weigh them very carefully. We will see that declaring people to be unconverted who claim to be Christians and are living good lives is forbidden by Christ in the New Testament. Since he forbids it, his disciples must not do it - however well qualified they may think they are, and however necessary it may seem to be. This is a judgement that God claims as his alone; we are forbidden to claim it for ourselves. Judging the hearts of men belongs only to him. 'Forgive and act; deal with each man according to all he does, since you [God] know his heart (for you alone know the hearts of all men.)' (1 Kings 8.39) It is not just the *motive* of men's hearts that we may not judge; we cannot judge the *state* of their hearts before God - that is, whether or not those who claim to be converted, are converted. This will be seen clearly in the following Scriptures: 1 Chr. 28:9; Ps. 7:9,10,11; Ps. 26; Prov 16:2, 17:3, 21:2; Job 2:23, 24,25; Rev. 2:22,23. This judging is also forbidden in Romans 14:4 ('Who are you to judge someone else's servant? To his own master he stands or falls.') and James 4:12 ('There is only one lawgiver and judge, the one who is able to save and destroy. But you - who are you to judge your neighbour?'); also 1 Cor. 4:3,4 ('I care very little if I am judged by you or by any human court; indeed, I do not even judge myself... It is the Lord who judges me').

This is reinforced by the commands not to indulge in that kind of judgement which belongs to the last day, as in 1 Cor 4:5 for example. ('Therefore judge nothing before the appointed time; wait till the Lord comes. He will bring to light what is hidden in darkness and will expose the motives of men's hearts. At that time each will receive his praise from God.')

Separating hypocrites, who have the form of godliness and talk like godly men, from the saints is separating the sheep from the goats - and this is what Judgement Day is for! It is therefore a great mistake for a man to take it upon himself to pass final judgement on who is genuine and who is not. We cannot draw a dividing line between true saints and hypocrites, or separate the sheep from the goats and the tares from the wheat; and we are forbidden to try. Many servants of the owner of this field think that they are capable of it! But the Lord says to them 'No, because while you are pulling the weeds, you may root up the wheat with them.' In the time of harvest, he will do the job properly - Mt. 13:28-30. In this parable those whose job it is to look after the crop are the same as those who must look after the vineyard in Luke 20. They are servants of the Lord of the harvest; they are ministers of the gospel. In our day we are seeing the parable of Matthew 13 fulfilled: the enemy has sowed weeds in the field while men slept (and the church has been through a long, sleepy time!); the crop is now growing as religion is revived; and some of the servants are saying 'Let us go and sort out the weeds.' I know that some men who have experienced something of the power of religion think they are well able to do this job; why, they only need to talk to a person for a few minutes and their minds are fully made up! But experience has shown me that this is wrong.

There was a time when I did not realise how unsearchable a man's heart is. Now, I am both less charitable, and more charitable, than I used to be. I see more things in the wicked that appear to counterfeit holiness, and more things in the godly that make them appear still carnal, and spiritually dead hypocrites, than I ever dreamed! The longer I live, the less I am surprised that God keeps to himself the right to judge the hearts of men, and orders that we leave this business alone until the harvest. I adore the wisdom of God, as well as his goodness to us, that he has not given this great work into the hands of such a poor, weak and dim-sighted creature! I am so full of blindness, pride, partiality, prejudice and deceitfulness of heart, that I rejoice that he has given this work to one who is infinitely more suited to it.

It is true that the conversation of some people, and the account they give of their experiences, is very encouraging. We cannot even think that they may not be children of God. We are obliged to think the best of them; yet we must allow the Scriptures to stand. They remind us that everything in the saint that belongs to the spiritual life is hidden. (Col 3:3,4) Their food is the hidden manna; they have meat to eat that others do not know about; a stranger cannot understand their joys. It is in the heart alone that the beauty of the inner self can be seen (1 Peter 3:4); and only God can see that heart. Christ has given them a new name, and they are the only ones who know it. (Rev. 2:17) The true Israelite is the one who is circumcised inwardly, and his praise belongs to God, not men. That is, only

God can tell that he is indeed a true Israelite, as the apostle makes clear by a similar expression in 1 Cor 4:5. Here he says that it is God's privilege to judge who is a true Christian, and he will do so at judgement day; he adds 'At that time each will receive his praise from God.'

The case of Judas is a remarkable warning. Though he had been so long among the rest of the disciples (and their experience was genuine) still they did not seem even to have imagined that he was not a true disciple until he revealed himself by wicked behaviour. The case of Ahitophel is also very remarkable. David did not suspect him, even though he was a wise and holy man. David knew the Scriptures very well; he knew more than all his teachers, more than the ancients even; he was very experienced and at the height of his powers. He was a great prophet, and intimately acquainted with Ahitophel. They were great friends, and close companions in religious and spiritual matters. Yet not only did David not realise that he was a hypocrite, he relied on him as a true saint. He relished spiritual communion with him; he regarded him as a great saint. More than any other man David made him his guide in spiritual matters. But Ahitophel was not a saint at all. He was a wicked man, a murderous vile wretch. 'Destructive forces are at work in the city; threats and lies never leave its streets. If an enemy were insulting me, I could endure it; if a foe were raising himself against me I could hide from him. But it is you, a man like myself, my companion, my close friend, with whom I once enjoyed sweet fellowship as we walked with the throng at the house of God.' (Psalm 55:11-14)

So it is quite wrong to imagine that men have the right and the ability to judge between those who appear to be Christians. No-one has a right to exclude any of these in any other way than by normal church discipline, which God has given to his church. I beg of those who are truly zealous for promoting the work of God to think hard about this. I am sure that those who have much to do with souls will eventually come to agree with me as their experience increases, even if they do not listen to me now.

4. Let us be careful of controversy. I would ask the friends of this glorious revival to avoid too much controversy. Too much debate is carried on with heat and anger. In particular, too much is said in public prayer and preaching about persecution. If persecution were ten times greater than it is, I still think it would be best not to say too much about it. Christians are to be like lambs, not apt to complain and cry too much when they are hurt. It is good for them to be dumb and not open the mouth, following the example of our dear Redeemer. They are not to be like pigs, that tend to squeal when they are touched. We should not be too ready to think and speak of fire from heaven when the Samaritans oppose us and will not welcome us into their villages. God's zealous ministers should think carefully about the instructions the apostle Paul gave to a zealous young minister, 2 Tim 2:24-26. 'The Lord's servant must not quarrel; instead, he must be kind to everyone, able to teach, not resentful. Those who oppose him he must gently instruct, in the hope that God will grant them repentance leading them to a knowledge of the truth, and that they will come to their senses and escape from the trap of the devil, who has taken them captive to do his will.'

Finally, I offer a few closing words of advice. I would humbly recommend to those that love the Lord Jesus Christ and want to advance his kingdom to pay careful attention to that excellent rule of wisdom he has given us, 'No-one sews a patch of unshrunk cloth on an old garment, for the patch will pull away from the garment, making the tear worse. Neither do men pour new wine into old wineskins. If they do, the skins will burst, the wine will run out and the wineskins will be ruined. No, they pour new wine into new wineskins, and both are preserved.' (Mt. 9:16,17) I am afraid that the wine is now running out in some parts of this land because men have not paid attention to those words. While it is true that I believe we

75

have insisted too much that there is one way of doing things in religious matters, and that this has led to much of our religion degenerating into mere formality - yet at the same time, we need to avoid those things which are too novel. They tend to shock and set people talking and arguing, and so hinder the progress of the power of true religion. It causes some to oppose the work, and occupies the minds of others, and puzzles many with doubts and scruples. As a result people swerve from the most important things, and turn aside to empty shells. So something which is very different from normal practice ought to be avoided, unless it is of great importance. By this we shall follow the example of Paul, who had the greatest success in spreading the power of true religion. 'To the Jews I became like a Jew, to win the Jews. To those under the law, I became like one under the law (though I myself am not under the law), so as to win those under the law. To those not having the law I became like one not having the law (though I am not free from God's law but am under Christ's law) so as to win those not having the law. To the weak I became weak, to win the weak. I have become all things to all men so that by all possible means I might save some. I do all this for the sake of the gospel, that I may share in its blessings.' (1 Cor. 9:20-23)

Sinners in the hands of an angry God

'In due time their foot will slip' - Deut. 32:35

In this verse, God threatens vengeance on the wicked and unbelieving Israelites. They were God's people. They knew God's law and had sacrifices for sin that he had appointed. They had seen God at work in miraculous ways. Yet in spite of all this, as verse 28 says, they had no spiritual discernment. They were like a garden which had only produced poisonous fruit in spite of all that the gardener had done, as the two previous verses say. The words I have chosen for my text ('In due time their foot will slip') imply the following four things about the punishment and destruction to which these wicked Israelites were exposed.

First, that they *were* exposed to destruction. They were like a person standing or walking in a slippery place, always in danger of falling. The very picture the text uses is of a foot sliding, and the same picture is used in Psalm 73:18 'Surely you place them on slippery ground; you cast them down to ruin.'

Second, it implies that their destruction could come suddenly, at any time. A man that walks in slippery places is always in danger of falling. He cannot tell whether he will stand or fall in the next moment; if he does fall, he falls at once without warning. Again, this is expressed in Psalm 73: 18,19: 'Surely you place them on slippery ground; you cast them down to ruin. How suddenly are they destroyed, completely swept away by terrors!'

Third, it is implied that they are liable to fall without anyone pushing them. A man standing or walking on slippery ground does not need to be pushed; his own weight is enough to cause him to fall.

Fourth, it is implied that the only reason they have not fallen already is that God's appointed time has not yet come. The text says that when that appointed time does come, their foot *will* slip. At that moment they will be left to fall. God will not hold them up in those slippery places any more. He will let them go, and the moment that he lets them go they will fall to destruction.

The point that I want to draw out from this text and apply to us is this: *The only thing that keeps wicked men out of hell for one moment, is that it pleases God to keep them out.* When I say it is the only thing, I mean that God is sovereign and does everything he wants. When I say that it pleases God, I mean that there is no other restraint on him. It would not be difficult for him to let that man fall. Let me explain a little further.

1. God does not lack the power to cast wicked men into hell at any moment. No one is strong enough to resist God. He is not only able to cast the wicked into hell, it would be a very easy thing for him to do. Sometimes an earthly ruler tries to subdue someone who has rebelled against him but finds it difficult. Perhaps the rebel has built a strong fortress for himself, or has a large number of followers. But it is not like that with God. No fortress is strong enough to defend any man from his power. No amount of enemies joining together can be strong enough to resist him. At the most, they are like great piles of light chaff in the path of a whirlwind, or like vast quantities of dry stubble in the path of devouring flames. We find it easy to tread on a worm crawling on the earth. We have no difficulty cutting a slender thread that holds a weight. It is as easy as that for God to cast his enemies into hell at any moment that he pleases. The earth itself trembles when he speaks; do we think that we can stand before him?

2. Wicked men deserve to be cast into hell. God is a just God; but his justice will not prevent him casting them into hell. On the contrary, justice cries out that their sins should be punished infinitely. God's justice says of ground that produces 'the vine of Sodom' (verse 32) 'Cut it down; why should it use up the soil?' (Lk. 13:7) God's sword is ready to strike at any moment; only God's will holds it back. It is God's mercy, not his justice, that prevents their foot slipping at this very moment.

3. They are already under a sentence of condemnation to hell. God's law is an unchangeable law of righteousness, and it has already pronounced the sentence. That sentence is 'Whoever does not believe stands condemned already' (John 3:18). Every unconverted man belongs in hell; we could say that it is his proper home. Jesus said to some men 'You are from below' (John 8:23) - and that is where they are heading! Justice demands that the sinner be cast into hell, and God's word promises that the proper time will come.

4. God is already angry with them, just as he will be when they are in hell. When the wicked are tormented in hell, it is because God is angry with them. The reason why some men do not fall into hell this very moment is *not* because God is not angry with them! Indeed, God is more angry with some that are alive at this moment and on the earth (and even in this congregation, listening to this sermon!) than he is with some who are already in the flames of hell. It is not that God does not care about their wickedness; already, his wrath burns against them. Already the pit is prepared, the fire is ready, the furnace is hot and able to receive them. God is not 'just like us', whatever we might imagine!

5. The devil is ready at this moment to pounce on them. He is ready to take them to be his own forever, as soon as God allows it. They belong to him; he has their souls in his possession and they are members of his kingdom. The Scripture tells us that they are his own possessions, Luke 11:21. The devils are like greedy, hungry lions that can see their prey but cannot, for the moment, reach it. It is God who holds them back. If he takes away his hand, they will immediately fall upon the souls of the wicked.

6. Wicked men already have hell within them. Every carnal man already has within himself the seeds of hell fire. There are such sins in his heart that, if God did not hold them back, they would burst out just as they do in the souls of the damned. The souls of the wicked are compared in Scripture to a troubled sea (Is. 57:20). At the moment, God uses his great power to hold back their wickedness; but if God withdraws that power, their wickedness will destroy everything. Sin is the ruin and misery of the soul; the corruptions of man's heart are boundless. If sin were not restrained by God's almighty power, it would immediately turn the soul into a fiery oven, a furnace of fire and brimstone.

7. Men are in danger, even when they think they are safe. Though a man may seem to be in good health, with no danger near him, yet he may step into eternity the very next moment! He may not be able to see any accident looming on the horizon, and yet it may be there. We all know from history and experience that this is so. There are so many things we never think of that may take a man out of this world. Unconverted men are walking over the pit of hell on a rotten plank, and there are so many places in the plank that are just too weak to bear their weight. If God wants to remove a man from life at any moment, there are so many ways to do it that he certainly does not need a miracle! And remember, everything is in God's control; every disease, every accident, every possible way of death is his to command.

8. All the care a man may take will not grant him a moment's extra life. Again, all our experience shows this to be true. A wise man dies just as easily as a foolish man; no amount of care, in the end, makes any difference. We know that, on average, the wise man lives no longer than the fool. This is what the

Scripture says: 'Like the fool, the wise man too must die.' (Eccl. 2:16)

9. However much a man may expect to escape hell, he will not escape it if he continues to reject Christ. Everyone who hears about hell imagines that, one way or another, he will escape it! He believes perhaps that his own goodness will save him. He trusts in good deeds that he has done, or that he is doing. Or possibly, he expects one day to do some good deeds that will deliver him from hell. And everyone imagines that he cannot fail! He may hear that only a few are saved, and that most people who have ever died have gone to hell already; but still he thinks he will succeed where others have failed. He is sure he will not be sent to that place of torment; he intends to make sure of it!

But such men are fools, and deluding themselves. When they trust their own deeds and plans, they are trusting shadows. It is true that most people who have died are now in hell; but it is not because they were more foolish than those who are now alive! It is not because they were not as careful, or because they did not make plans to avoid hell! If we could ask them, one at a time, how many expected to go to hell when they heard about it, they would surely say 'No: I was determined to be so careful; I made such careful plans; I thought I would be good enough to escape hell. But death came to me so suddenly! I was not expecting it; it came like a thief. God's wrath was too quick for me. I was a fool! Even while I was dreaming of the things I would do to escape hell, sudden death claimed me for its own.'

10. God is not obliged to keep any unconverted person out of hell one more moment. He has not made any promise anywhere that obliges him to do this. He has not promised eternal life, nor has he promised to save from eternal death, anyone except through faith in Christ. There is a covenant of grace; God has made many great and gracious promises. But those promises only apply to those who share in that covenant; that

81

is, to those who believe them and trust in the Lord Jesus Christ. Those who do not believe and trust have no share at all in these promises. Until a man believes in Christ, God is under no obligation to keep him from eternal hell for even a moment.

The sum of what I have said so far is this: all unconverted men are held in God's hands over the pit of hell. Everyone by nature deserves that hell; God is angry with sinners and, until they trust in Christ, there is no safety for them. There is nothing that they can take hold of; the only thing that keeps them out of hell is that God's time has not yet come; but it is coming, and their foot will slip.

Section 2: Application

This is an awesome subject! Because of that, it may be useful for waking the unconverted up from their sins. Be sure; what I have described is true of every single person who is not a true Christian believer. A miserable eternity, a lake of burning brimstone, is stretched out underneath you. Already the flames of God's anger burn hot and bright; hell's mouth is open wide ready to receive you, and there is nothing for you to stand on, nothing for you to take hold of. There is nothing between you and hell but the air; only God's pleasure and will holds you up.

You may not be aware of this. You know (of course!) that you are not in hell, but you do not realise that it is because of God. You see other reasons instead; your own good health, the care you take and so on. But in the end these things count for nothing; if God should withdraw his hand they could not keep you from falling any more than thin air can hold up a man!

It is your own sin that makes you heavy, like lead. If God should let you go, the weight of it would take you to hell. Your good health, your own carefulness, and even your very best righteousness, could not keep you up any more than a spider's web could catch a rock! If it were not for the sovereign pleasure of God, the earth would not hold you a moment. Even the creation itself objects to your sin, and groans with it. The sun itself would refuse to shine on you if it could, rather than continue to give you light as you sin and serve Satan. The earth that provides food and drink for you would stop if it could; for you use these good gifts to feed your own lusts. The very air you breathe is reluctant to be used by you, because it keeps you alive to serve God's enemies. All that God has made is good, and was made for men to serve God with. It is not happy to be used for other purposes. The world itself would vomit you out, if God did not prevent it. There are storm clouds over your head at this moment; clouds that do not carry rain, but the wrath of God ready to fall upon you; it is only God who prevents it falling. Hurricanes of God's anger are ready to blow; yet for the moment, God holds them back. If he did not, you would be destroyed as easily as a whirlwind destroys chaff on a threshing-floor in the summer.

The wrath of God is like a great lake held back by a mighty dam; behind that dam the waters get higher and higher, deeper and deeper, until a door is opened. The longer the stream has been dammed, the faster and stronger will it flow when that door is opened. Yes, it is true; God has not judged you for your sin so far. But your guilt is increasing all the time, and every day you deserve more and more of God's anger. The waters are rising, growing ever stronger! Nothing holds them back, except God; if he should withdraw his hand for a moment, the flood-gate would fly open, and all the floods of God's wrath would rush upon you with omnipotent power. Even if you were ten thousand times stronger than you are, or ten thousand times stronger than the strongest devil in hell, you would not be able to stand before that flood.

God's anger is like a bow already bent, with an arrow on the string. It is justice that aims the arrow at your heart and bends the bow, and only God stops the arrow flying. Yet God is angry! He has not promised to hold back that arrow, and any moment it could fly. All those of you that have never been converted by the mighty power of God's Spirit on your souls; all those of you that were never born again and made new creatures; all those of you that have not been raised from the death of sin - you are in the hands of an angry God. However many times you may have reformed your life; however religious you may have been; it is not enough. Only God's pleasure keeps you, at this moment, from everlasting destruction. You may not believe this at the moment; but, eventually, you will be convinced that what I say is true.. You will be fully convinced! Some of your friends and neighbours have already died; they were once just like you, and then death came on them suddenly. They were not expecting it; they were saying 'Peace and safety' - but now they know that they were trusting thin air and empty shadows to save them.

The God who at this moment holds you over hell's pit (as we might hold a spider over a fire) hates you [1] and is dreadfully provoked by your sin. His anger burns like a fire. He sees you as worthy of nothing else, except to be cast into the fire. He is too pure even to tolerate you in his sight. You have offended him far more than any rebel has ever offended his master - yet it is his hand that holds you from the flames. It is only because of him that you did not go to hell last night. It is only because of him that you woke this morning, and have not been cast into hell since! Even while you have been sitting here this morning in worship, you have been provoking him further by your sinful attitudes; yet still his hand, only his hand, holds you from hell. At this moment, even now, it is only his hand that holds you.

O sinner! Think about the awful danger you are in; remember that hell is a blazing furnace of wrath, it is a wide and bottomless pit. Remember that you are held over it in the very hands of God, an angry God. There are many in hell at this moment that God is angry with; remember he is just as angry with you! Picture yourself being held by a slender thread, and the flames of hell already licking at that thread; any moment it will burn through and you will fall. Yet you have no Saviour; there is nothing you can hold on to, nothing you can trust in, nothing that you have ever done or can ever do that will save you or persuade God to spare you one more moment.

This is such a serious subject, I want you to think particularly about the following things:

First think about just who it is that is angry with you. We are speaking about the wrath of the infinite God. If it were only the wrath of a man, even the most powerful man in the world, it would not matter nearly so much! Men may fear greatly the anger of kings, particularly those who are absolute monarchs and have the lives of their subjects in their power. So the Bible says 'A king's wrath is like the roar of a lion; he who angers him forfeits his life.' (Prov. 20:2) Some earthly kings have devised horrible things to torture those subjects who anger them. Yet the greatest king who ever lived, however great he is, however powerful, is feeble when compared with the great and almighty Creator and King of heaven and earth. An earthly king is like a grasshopper by comparison with God, and can do little to hurt. Both their love and their hatred are insignificant; they hardly matter. The anger of the great King of Kings is much greater than theirs, just as his majesty is greater than theirs. Remember the words of the Lord Jesus: 'I tell you my friends, do not be afraid of those who kill the body and after that can do no more. But I will show you whom you should fear: Fear him who, after the killing of the body, has power to throw you into hell. Yes, I tell you, fear him.' (Lk. 12:4,5)

Second, remember that it is the *fury* of his wrath that threatens you. The Bible often speaks about the anger of God; for example, Is. 59:18 'According to what they have done, so will he repay wrath to his enemies.' Is. 66:15 is another example: 'See the Lord is coming with fire and his chariots are like a whirlwind; he will bring down his anger with fury and his rebuke with flames of fire.' There are many other places like this, and they culminate in Revelation 19:15 where we read of 'the winepress of the fury of the wrath of God Almighty.'

These are awesome, terrifying words! If it had just said 'the wrath of God' that would have been terrible enough; but it is 'the fury of the wrath of God.' The fury of God! How terrifying that is! Who could find words to describe it! But there is still more, for it is ' the fury of the wrath of God *Almighty.*' This implies that this display of his anger will reveal much of his almighty power. It is to say that omnipotence itself is enraged, and so God's almighty power is called on as men exert their own strength when they are angry. Oh, what then will be the results! What will happen to those poor creatures who must suffer it! Who can stand against this!

Those of you that hear this, but are not yet converted, think about this carefully. If God is going to punish with the fury of his wrath, it clearly implies that there will be no pity. There will be no relief. Even when God sees how much you are suffering, and how weak you are, and that you are, as it were, in infinite gloom, he will still not stop. Mercy will not intervene; there will be no moderation; the fierce hurricane of his wrath will not turn aside at all. The only limits to your suffering will be this: that *you will not suffer at all beyond what strict justice requires.* He will not restrain himself just because you find his wrath hard to bear! 'I will deal with them in anger; I will not look on them with pity or spare them. Although they shout in my ears, I will not listen to them.' (Ezek. 8:18)

God is not cruel; he is a merciful God. Right at this moment, he is ready to have mercy on you. This is a day of mercy; if you cry now for mercy, be encouraged! He will hear. But once the day of mercy is past, the saddest cries and shrieks will be useless. You will be lost. There will be nothing else for God to do with you, than to punish you. You will continue to exist only for this reason: as an object of wrath prepared for destruction. Far from being full of pity at their condemnation, Scripture says God himself laughs and mocks. (Proverbs 1:25,26)

Think about these awesome words of Scripture: ' I have trodden the winepress alone; from the nations no-one was with me. I trampled them in my anger and trod them down in my wrath; their blood spattered my garments and I stained all my clothing.' (Is. 63:3) No words could show more clearly these three things: contempt, hatred and fierce wrath. If you cry to God then to pity you, he will not; instead, he will tread you underfoot. He knows that you cannot bear it, but it will not stop him; he will crush you under his feet without mercy, and your blood (as it were) will spatter his garments.

Third, remember that the suffering of hell is designed to show what God's anger is like. It is God's purpose to demonstrate to all creation just how great his love is; it is also his purpose to show how terrible his wrath is. Sometimes earthly kings want to do this; they show how great their anger is by the fierce punishments they inflict on their enemies. Nebuchadnezzar is one example. He was a proud king of the Chaldean empire, and wanted to show how great his anger was towards Shadrach, Meshech and Abednego. So he gave the instructions that the furnace should be heated seven times hotter than normal - that is, to the highest temperature human ingenuity could manage. God too wants to show the greatness of his anger by the sufferings of his enemies: 'What if God, choosing to show his wrath and make his power known, bore with great patience the objects of wrath, prepared for destruction?' (Rom. 9:22) Because this is his purpose, we may be sure that he will do it well! When his wrath is at last shown to the universe, the whole universe will be able so see just how great it is. 'The peoples will be burned as if to lime; like cut thornbushes they will be set ablaze. You who are far away, hear what I have done; you who are near, acknowledge my power! The sinners in Zion are terrified; trembling grips the godless.' (Is. 33:12-14)

This is what will happen to you, if you remain unconverted. The infinite power of God Almighty will be demonstrated to the whole universe by your sufferings. You will be tormented in the presence of the holy angels and of the Lamb himself; and when you are suffering like this, those in heaven will see. Then they will know what the fury and wrath of Almighty God is.

Then they shall worship him for his great power and majesty: "'From one New Moon to another and from one Sabbath to another, all mankind will come and bow down before me" says the Lord. "And they will go out and look upon the dead bodies of those who rebelled against me; their worm will not die, nor will their fire be quenched, and they will be loathsome to all mankind."' (Is. 66:23,24)

Fourth, remember that this wrath is *everlasting*. It would be unbearable to experience the fury of the wrath of Almighty God for a moment; but you must endure it for ever -if you are unconverted. There will be no end to the terrible suffering. When you look forward, you will see a long eternity. It is so long that you cannot imagine it; it will amaze your inmost being, and fill you with despair. You will know for certain that long ages are before you; millions of millions of ages; and through all those ages you must suffer God's almighty vengeance. When you have suffered that vengeance for all those ages, you will know that you have experienced only the tiniest part of eternity. Your punishment will indeed be infinite. Who can express what a soul will feel like in such circumstances! All that we can possibly say about it gives only a feeble idea; the truth is inexpressible. It is inconceivable. Who knows the power of God's anger!

How dreadful it is to live every day, every hour, in danger of this great wrath, this infinite misery! But that is the dismal truth about every single person in this congregation who has not been born again. However moral you may be, however religious, however strict you are; if you have not been born again, you are lost! Oh, that you would think about it, whether you are young or old! There is reason to believe that many who are in this congregation now, who are hearing this sermon, will experience this misery for all eternity. We do not know who they are, or where they are sitting, or what they are thinking. Perhaps they are feeling very comfortable at this moment. They hear all these things, but it does not worry them. Even now, they are sure I am talking about somebody else!

If we knew that one person in this congregation, just one, would have to endure hell for ever, how awful that would be to think of! If we knew who it was, how terrible it would be just to see them! Surely the rest of us would weep bitterly over him! But it is not just one! There are many, I am sure, who will remember this sermon in hell itself!

And some people, let us be sure, may well be in hell in a very short time, even before this year is out. In fact, some people who are now feeling quite well, quite secure, may well be in hell before tomorrow morning! Even those who stay out of hell the longest, will be there very soon indeed, unless you are converted. Your damnation has not fallen asleep; it will come swiftly and, perhaps, suddenly. The surprising thing is that you are not in hell already! Some people you knew, who were no worse than you, are already suffering hell's pains. Yet you are alive; you are in the house of God. You have an opportunity to be saved! How much the poor damned souls in hell would give for the opportunity you now have!

What a great opportunity you now have - an extraordinary opportunity! The doors of mercy have been flung wide open by the Lord Jesus Christ. He is calling with a loud clear voice to sinners, and many are coming to him. Many are pressing in to the kingdom of God. People come daily from the east and the west, from the north and the south. Many that were only recently as lost as you are now rejoicing with unspeakable joy. Their hearts are full of love to the Christ who has loved them and washed them from their sins in his own blood. They are rejoicing in the hope of the glory of God. How terrible it is to be left behind in such a day! To see so many others enjoying a great feast while you are starving! To see others rejoicing and singing for joy, when your own heart is full of sorrow! How can you stay like this one moment longer? Don't you know that your souls are as precious as those of the people at Suffield[2], where every day great numbers flock to Christ?

There are many here who have lived a long time and are still not born again. They are strangers to God's promises; they

89

have done nothing all their lives but add to the wrath they must experience. Oh, sirs, what danger you are in! Your guilt is great; your hearts are very hard. Do you not see that most people of your age are being by-passed by God's mercy at the moment? You need to wake up! Wake up before it is too late! You cannot bear the fury of the wrath of Almighty God!

There are others here, both men and women, who are still quite young. Will you neglect this great opportunity that God has given, even though so many of your own age are taking advantage of it? There is a special opportunity for you at the moment! But if you let it pass, it will soon be the same for you as it is for others, who spent all their youths in sin. Now they are so blind, and their hearts are so hard!

And children - some of you are still unconverted. Do you not realise that you are going to hell, to bear the dreadful anger of God? He is angry with you now, every day and every night. Why be content to be children of the devil, when so many other children in the land are converted? *They* have become holy and happy, the children of the King of Kings.

Now let everyone who is still not a true believer listen to the loud calls of God's word. You are hanging over the pit of hell, whether you are old or young, man or woman. But today is the acceptable year of the Lord; you may be saved! If in a day like this you harden your heart, your guilt will be much greater! God seems to be gathering in his elect quickly in all parts of the land. So many are being converted that it is probable that most of those adults who ever will be saved, will be saved within a short time from now. It will be as it was when the Spirit came on the Jews in the apostles' days; the elect will receive it, and the rest will be blinded. If you should be blinded, then for all eternity you will curse this day! You will curse the day that you were born; you will wish that you had died and gone to hell before this great revival began. It is now as it was in the days of John the Baptist: the axe is laid at the root of the trees. Every tree that does not bear good fruit will be chopped down and thrown into the fire.

Let everyone that is not a true believer, now wake up and flee from the coming wrath! Undoubtedly the wrath of Almighty God is hanging over a great part of this congregation! It is like Sodom, and God's word says 'Flee for your lives! Don't look back. Flee to the mountains, or you will be swept away!'

[1] Edwards says this very clearly, yet it is a strange idea to modern ears, who are used to hearing that 'God hates the sin but loves the sinner.' Yet consider the following Scriptures: Lev. 20:23, Ps. 5:4-6, 11:5. One modern writer says about these verses 'The last phrase could hardly be more emphatic. God hates the sinner with every fibre of his being.' He also points out '[There are] thirty-three places in the Bible where God's hatred is expressed. In twelve, he is said to hate sinners' actions... but in the other twenty-one he is said to hate the sinner.' (John Blanchard, 'Whatever happened to hell?' pp 170-171)

[2] A town nearby.

Appendix: Some Notes on Books

A great deal of literature about Edwards and the Great Awakening is now available; not all of it is reliable! At the same time, we are greatly blessed by access to large amounts of Edwards' own writings.

Biography

The best biography of Edwards currently available is that by Iain H. Murray, 'Jonathan Edwards, a New Biography.' (Banner of Truth, 1987)

Edwards' 'Works'

Two large volumes of Edwards' own writings are available from Banner of Truth. Edwards is not easy to read, but repays every effort. As an interpreter of revival and religious experience he has no equal. His two major writings on revival are both contained in those volumes. 'The Distinguishing Marks of a Work of the Spirit of God' dates from 1741, and this current volume is based on that. The other work 'A Treatise concerning Religious Affections' dates from 1746 and is also available from Grace Publications in simplified form as 'The Experience that Counts.'

'Distinguishing Marks' and 'Religious Affections.'

These two works are both based on sermons preached by Edwards, and both have their origin in the same period. 'Religious Affections' however was published five years after

'Distinguishing Marks' and the contemporary situation brings some differences.

From the very beginning of the revival, Edwards was aware of mistakes and lack of wisdom in some people who supported it. In 'Distinguishing Marks' he is concerned to prove that some errors do not prove that God is at work; he succeeds brilliantly. By the time 'Religious Affections' was published, these errors had become much more serious and are, in Edwards' opinion, damaging to true Christianity. He fights two battles therefore; first, arguing that those who think he over-emphasises emotion have not really understand Christianity. Second, he argues that some have gone too far, and demonstrated that their own religion is counterfeit. Both works are vital if we are to have a balanced understanding, not only of his own day, but of our own.